If you know someone who's had an abortion . . .

Do you have a friend or relative wh ortion? Maybe you were involved . . maybe you were in the waitin . maybe she confided in you lon und out, you have picked up this l you've seen her sadness and wondere help.

Your best gift to her will be your love and prayers. She may or may not be ready to work through her pain. But perhaps this book can be a resource—something she can tuck in a drawer and pull out some rainy day when the issue has become too hard to avoid. When that day comes, be ready with a list of the post-abortion ministries and resources in your community to suggest. These can usually be found in the "abortion alternatives" section of your Yellow Pages. But most of all, be ready with your unconditional support. God bless you in your desire to help.

If you have had an abortion . . .

Perhaps you are thinking, "Okay, so I had an abortion. But that is in my past. Do I really need to be healed?"

Some women seemingly never need to work through any kind of healing process. But for many of us, the memory of abortion lies like a hidden infection within, weakening and impairing us in ways we may have never realized were related. Is that true for you? See if you recognize yourself in some of the following questions. (A more complete list appears on pages 16-20.)

- Do you feel reluctant to talk about the subject of abortion, or do you feel guilt, anger, or sorrow when discussing your own abortion?
- Do you tend to think of your life in terms of "before" and "after" the abortion?

- Do you have lingering feelings of resentment or anger toward people involved in your abortion, such as the baby's father, friends, or your parents?
- Have you found yourself either avoiding relationships or becoming overly dependent in them since the abortion? Are you overly protective of any children you have now?
- Have you begun or increased use of drugs or alcohol since the abortion, or do you have an eating disorder?
- Have you felt a vague sort of emptiness, a deep sense of loss, or had prolonged periods of depression?
- Do you sometimes have nightmares, flashbacks, or hallucinations relating to the abortion?

If so, it is likely you are experiencing Post-Abortion Syndrome. Relief can be found for you in the pages of this book. We invite you to read on and find the peace you had forgotten existed.

How to read this book . . .

The peace you search for will come, but it may not come quickly or all at once. Read this book slowly. You may read a chapter, then spend days or weeks processing what you have read. Writing is a form of self-expression and self-examination and self-therapy. Many times it is difficult to know what you are thinking and feeling until you put it in writing. Just remember, there are no boundaries, no rights or wrongs about how or what to write. It may help to keep a journal of your ideas, thoughts, prayers during this time. The *Healing Place* section at the end of each chapter will help you get started. Others of you may need to find a person to confide in, someone who can be trusted with your deepest fears and secrets. A friend, perhaps, or a professional counselor can help in the process. For help in finding someone to talk to, give the Crisis Pregnancy Center in your town a call. (See "abortion alternatives" in the Yellow Pages directory.)

"The testimonies in *Her Choice to Heal,* interwoven with God's beautiful promises, are straight forward, powerful, and moving. Sydna and Joan greatly challenge women to dismantle their walls of denial and begin the healing journey, then offer them a way to do just that through this book. I highly recommend their story to bring understanding and hope, not only to women who have had abortions, but also to other abortion "survivors"—fathers, grandparents, and siblings of aborted babies—who face similar journeys from denial through reconciliation."

Margaret H. Hartshorn, Ph.D.
Heartbeat International

"Millions of women carry the unspeakable heartache of a past abortion. Few have found the forgiveness and healing they long for. *Her Choice to Heal* offers a breakthrough for this generation of hurting women. Sydna Massé and Joan Phillips show the way home—from a place of brokenness and despair to a place of healing and hope in the presence of Jesus Christ."

Guy Condon
President
Care Net

"Post-abortion has become a major issue for the pro-life community. Sydna and Joan are well qualified to write *Her Choice to Heal* from personal experience as well as their experience and responsibilities at Focus on the Family."

Anne Pierson
Executive Director
Loving & Caring Inc.

"Even though I've never had an abortion, this book has helped me. . . A must read for post-abortive women."

Norma McCorvey
(Roe of Roe v. Wade)
Author, *Won By Love*

her choice to heal

finding spiritual and emotional peace after abortion

Sydna Massé & Joan Phillips

For Her. For God. For Real.
faithfulwoman.com

Chariot Victor Publishing
Cook Communications, Colorado Springs, CO 80918
Cook Communications, Paris, Ontario
Kingsway Communications, Eastbourne, England

Edited by Glenda Schlahta
Design by Big Cat Studios, Inc.

First printing, 1998
Printed in the United States of America
4 3 Printing/Year 02

Library of Congress Cataloging-in-Publication Data

Massé, Sydna
Her choice to heal/Sydna Massé and Joan Phillips.
p. cm.
Includes bibliographical references.
ISBN 1-56476-734-5
1. Abortion—Psychological aspects. 2. Abortion—Religious aspects—Chrisitanity. I. Phillips, Joan. II. Title.
RG734.M37 1998 98-27035
618.8'8'019--dc21 CIP

This book is lovingly dedicated to our children:
Jesse, Robert, Faith, and Hope—
may your memory live forever in our hearts.

acknowledgments

Our deepest thanks go to our families, whose personal encouragement has enabled this book to be written. We are grateful to each person who has assisted us in this project and for the prayers of the faithful that have inspired our work.

Our gratitude goes to the Colorado Springs Pregnancy Center. Without the compassion, understanding, and support of the trained counselors there, neither of us would have had the courage to face the truth nor have found healing and peace. Our prayers go out to crisis pregnancy centers everywhere that have pioneered post-abortion ministry services and compassionately reached out to women. May God greatly bless your efforts.

We are also most appreciative to Dr. Vincent Rue for sharing years of research and analysis with us. Our dear friend Teri Reisser, along with her husband, Dr. Paul Reisser, graciously allowed the use of their publication, *Identifying and Overcoming Postabortion Syndrome*. Linda Cochrane, author of *Forgiven and Set Free Bible Study*, has become our close friend. We are humbled by the generosity of these people. Without their dedication and compassion for the post-abortive woman the truth might never be known of the devastating affects abortion may have on the human race.

We would like to thank Dr. James C. Dobson of Focus on the Family. You were one of the first Christian leaders to publicly recognize the pain a woman can feel after an abortion. Because of your faithfulness in this area, many of us are now strong members of the pro-life movement.

To Rev. H.B. London, Jr., thank you, dear friend. You allowed us to benefit from your wonderful pastoral leadership when we first began our work with crisis pregnancy centers. Thank you for believing in us.

For the staff at Chariot Victor Publishing—especially Lee Hough who gave us godly insight and wisdom, along with many heartfelt prayers—we couldn't have done this without you!

Finally to the most important people in our lives—our husbands, Tom and Bill, as well as our sons, Bruce, Michael, Daniel, Mark, Brian, Steven, and Daniel—we could never have accomplished this without your support. Thank you so much.

table of contents

prologue

Since the 1973 Roe versus Wade Supreme Court case which legalized abortion, there have been close to thirty-five million abortions—and for every one of those abortions, there is a mother who found herself faced with a painful decision and the physical and emotional stress of the procedure itself. At first, for many women, there is relief. They no longer are faced with the problem of an unplanned or unwanted pregnancy. For months and even years, the only apparent truth is that she made the right decision for that time in her life.

But underlying the feelings of relief are often other feelings that are quite unexplained. Feelings of loss, guilt, and confusion seem to persist for no apparent reason. Life seems to be a roller coaster of emotion, with extreme highs and lows. Many women turn to substance abuse to ease or hide this inexplicable pain that persistently nags at their souls.

Other women avoid the pain by undergoing an emotional desensitization, or "numbing." Working hard to keep their feelings in check, they experience neither highs nor lows. For some women this creates a callousness, a lack of sensitivity which hampers their ability to form and maintain close interpersonal relationships.

Although abortion is legally and socially acceptable, there is still a stigma attached to it. Most women never talk about their abortion and try not to think about it. It is usually considered best forgotten by all involved. Fearful of being exposed, judged, condemned and/or rejected, it's common for a woman to find herself withdrawing deeper within herself, telling herself that as long as no one finds out, she can go on with life as if nothing ever happened.

But something did happen. Her body was invaded and violated. A child was ripped from the sanctuary of her womb, a place that is supposed to be the ultimate in safety and security. And, as much as she wants to believe that she has had a mere lump of tissue removed in a simple medical procedure, some deep part of her knows that it is not so. Although well-meaning people assured her that the ordeal would soon be behind her, for most women, that is not the case. Most will suffer deeply and silently and, in broad-spread ways, a set of symptoms known as Post-Abortion Syndrome. Research by David Reardon of the Elliott Institute in 1987 has shown that, regardless of age, family size, race, marital status, or number of abortions, of those surveyed:

- 61 percent experience flashbacks
- 54 percent have anniversary reactions
- 33 percent feel suicidal
- 78 percent have feelings of diminished control of their lives
- 52 percent experience difficulty developing and maintaining relationships
- 49 percent begin or increase drug use[1]

Ironically, though women seek out abortion as a solution to stressful circumstances, abortion itself can become a contributor to long-lasting stress of a different kind.

As two of those who have experienced first-hand the lasting effects of abortion, we believe that Post-Abortion Syndrome does, indeed, exist, but that it can be overcome. To the woman who is struggling, we would like to extend you our compassion—as well as a supporting arm to guide you along the way to healing through the pages of this book. You are in our prayers as you begin your journey toward peace.

introduction

We are everywhere. We are in churches. We are in shopping centers. We are in grocery stores. We are in daycare centers. We are high school dropouts. We are high school graduates. We have bachelor degrees, masters and Ph.D. degrees. We work well below our level of capability. We work at the top level of corporations and government.

We are women who have experienced abortion.

We have a secret we cannot share. If people knew the truth about us they would not like us, love us, or associate with us. We have committed a sin so horrendous we believe it is unforgivable.

The unforgivable sin. The sin we carry inside our hearts. The sin we believe stamps a scarlet letter **A** on our forehead and soul. . . .

Society is not going to punish us. We punish ourselves with self-destructive habits: drugs, alcohol, eating disorders, sexual dysfunctions, suicide attempts or completions, abusive relationships.

Years later something snaps and we can no longer bear the burden of our sin. We confess. Perhaps tentatively, carefully, cautiously, discreetly, prudently to a friend, a loved one, a boyfriend or a husband. The pain, the pain . . .

In *Her Choice to Heal*, you will find women who have lived with that pain and found help, healing, and hope. They have learned they can recover from their abortions and even find peace.

Perhaps you have experienced abortion, perhaps you want to help a friend or loved one heal from the pain of abortion, or perhaps you want to better understand this issue. I encourage you to read *Her Choice to Heal* and recognize there is hope in the recovery process when we understand and recognize the loss of our child, perhaps name that child and mourn, grieve that loss, and accept God's forgiveness. Then we are free to forgive ourselves and go on to the hope Christ offered on the cross and still offers today.

My friends, we have all been touched by abortion in some way. As you read, ask the Lord how He wants to use this book in your life.

Carol Everett
President
Life Network

CHAPTER 1

our stories

Sydna's Story

It was my second semester of college at a private Christian university. I was missing my high-school boyfriend, and I had yet to make any friends among the girls in my dorm. My relationship with my mother was strained, and my parents' divorce years earlier had left me with almost no relationship with my dad. I was miserable at school, and desperately lonely. So when Alan* began to pursue a relationship with me, he seemed like my knight in shining armor.

I knew he was mainly attracted to me for my dark red hair. But then again, I was mainly attracted to him for the escape he provided from my loneliness. There was only one catch to the relationship—sex. I knew I'd have to provide that if I wanted to keep Alan around. Since I wasn't a virgin anyway, it didn't seem to be too high a price to pay. Still, using birth control made the whole thing seem too deliberate . . . and that summer, I found myself pregnant.

* Name has been changed.

Alan went with me to get the pregnancy test at the local Planned Parenthood clinic. At least, he drove me to the clinic. Once there, I was on my own; he waited in the car. As I waited for the test results, knowing the potential outcome, I dared to hope Alan might support me in this pregnancy. Deep inside, I was beginning to fall in love with my unborn baby. My whole world turned upside down when the counselor joyfully confirmed that I was pregnant.

But one look at Alan's face, as I relayed the truth, dashed those hopes. He exploded in anger. "If you are thinking of continuing this pregnancy, Sydna, let me lay out the situation for you. First of all, I will tell everyone it's not mine, and I will not allow my parents to help you. Your mother will have a nervous breakdown and probably put you in the streets. The school doesn't allow pregnant students so you'll be kicked out. You'll be on your own! It doesn't look like you have much choice."

Once again, I felt hopelessly alone and backed into a corner. Abortion was my only option; it seemed there was no other choice. I also thought that if his father was unwilling to love him, this child would be better off not being brought into the world.

To survive, I began to distance myself from any maternal feelings I might have toward my unborn child. Since I was only four weeks along, I was informed that I would have to wait three weeks to have the abortion to ensure that the procedure was successful. As I waited for the day of the abortion, I forced myself to view this child as the enemy that would end my mother's sanity and my security.

That horrible Saturday in September, Alan once again waited in the car. Deep loneliness overwhelmed me as I climbed the stairs to the abortion clinic, but I felt there was no turning back. As the instruments entered my body, searing pain enveloped my consciousness—Alan had not wanted to pay for anesthesia. Instinctively, I began to fight the doctor, and his grip on my thighs tightened. Intense cramping began as I visualized my uterus being ripped from inside out. I knew that I was screaming loudly. Within several minutes it was over, and the doctor's grip relaxed.

When I entered the clinic, I had felt like my heart was breaking. With each step down those four flights of stairs my heart got colder and harder. On the way home, Alan handed me a joint, and with it a new way of life. Armed with birth control pills from the clinic and drugs from Alan, whose shining armor was by now thoroughly tarnished, I began drowning my feelings with drugs and promiscuity. It was a lifestyle that would continue for many years.

Joan's Story

In January of 1976, I was married to my high-school sweetheart and the mother of two sons. I had turned twenty-three in December, and my birthday found me miserable. The loving, attentive class clown that I had married had turned into an obsessive, jealous, violent monster. I lived in fear, and my life was like a prison. I could go nowhere, talk to no one without him. I was allowed only to go to my mom's to do the laundry. He even did the grocery shopping because he was so worried about me meeting someone. I lost contact with all my girlfriends from high school. My socialization came from my children or his friends who were over on a nightly basis, drinking and drugging. I cooked for all of them, listened to their vulgar and chauvinistic conversations, then cleaned up their messes the next day. All the while I remained the meek, submissive little wife who didn't talk back. I knew what was good for me.

The first time I had talked back to Bob I was out cold from his fist. When I came to, I saw stars circling around my head. My oldest son, nine months at the time, was screaming over me. Bob bragged to all his friends that night. "Joanie knows when to be quiet. She saw stars today." I was humiliated.

After four years of marriage and the abuse that came with it, I was weary of walking on eggshells and anticipating the next blow.

When I discovered I was pregnant for the third time, Mark was two and Brian was six months. Resolved to have another baby, I decided to make the best of it . . . but my decision changed when Bob came home drunk and began to throw me around. He put his fist through our television and then ran toward me. I dashed for the door but was not quick enough to escape his rage. He grabbed me by the neck and beat my head against the wall. When a neighbor called the police, I gathered my sons and left.

The next day I made an appointment for an abortion. I had decided that it would not be fair to bring another child into such a hostile environment. The child would be much better off not knowing what he had missed. I was doing this child a favor. Besides, according to what I was hearing, it wasn't really a baby *yet*—just a blob of tissue. And it was a legal option. Certainly the Supreme Court must know when a baby is a baby!

The abortion itself was a blur. I remember little apart from the nurse who held my hand and waking up in the recovery room. All the same, something seemed different. I felt as if I was on the outside, looking in. Inside I was screaming, "I want out! What is wrong with me? Am I crazy? Why am I feeling this way? Somebody help me!" But no one helped because they could not hear my silent screams.

The abortion changed me. As troubled as my marriage was already, Bob and I then became separated by a much deeper chasm. I was no longer terrified of him. I was indifferent to what he thought or did because down deep inside, I just didn't care about anything anymore. Soon afterward, I gathered the courage to leave him for good. I put my boys and myself on a plane to Colorado, where a friend and a job were waiting for me.

Our new life was good. I worked hard in my new job, and my bosses seemed to appreciate me—one in particular. Chuck*, though

* Name has been changed.

married and old enough to be my father, began to make advances toward me. I succumbed to his attention and thought I was falling in love with him. He told me he loved me too, and I believed him. We began a secret (or so I thought) relationship that would last two years—and through two pregnancies. He insisted on abortions both times. After all, he reminded me, he couldn't marry me. I'd have to quit my job and go on welfare, and would that be fair to my other children?

The first abortion, in March of 1980, was relatively fast and painless. Since I knew what to expect, I was not surprised at the cramping. After it was over, Chuck came into the room and kissed me. I loved him so much. It was all worth it for him. I couldn't lose him. Then he drove me home.

I stayed home for two days, then returned to work. Initially I was depressed and very emotional. I cried at the drop of a hat and didn't understand why. If I wasn't pregnant anymore, I shouldn't be having symptoms like raging hormones or mood swings. "What is wrong with me?" I kept asking myself. I clung to Chuck. I hardly wanted to let go when it was time for us to part. The numbness was setting in again. I felt as if I was on the outside, looking in at the world. The only time I felt anything at all was when I was with Chuck or smoking pot. And smoking pot was becoming more and more of a habit.

During this time I worked hard and cared for my sons. I wanted to be an outstanding salesperson and a great mother. I taught the boys to play ball and ride bikes. We went hiking and camping and maintained a very busy schedule. But I was on an emotional roller coaster. I performed to perfection, wearing the mask of the self-assured, liberated woman by day. At night the mask would come off. I would put the kids to bed, smoke my pot until I couldn't see, cry for no reason until the tears were gone, and wonder what was wrong with me. Was I going crazy?

My feelings for Chuck eventually began to wane. He could not understand my emotionalism. I couldn't get high around him, and I wanted to be high almost all the time now. I knew that if I could just be stoned I would feel no pain. The only problem was I did not know where that pain was coming from.

Besides, I was starting to doubt Chuck's love for me. Was he just another man who only wanted a passing fancy? He had said numerous times that he loved me. Why was I feeling so insecure lately?

But we continued to see each other, and by the following October I was pregnant again. There was hardly any discussion about it, except to set the appointment. Chuck had the nerve to ask if it could be someone else's child. That hurt. I had actually been faithful to him! A married man!

Again Chuck drove me to the abortion appointment. Again he waited. But this abortion was different; the physical pain was excruciating. I couldn't bear it. I screamed and tried to get up but was pushed back down. The doctor yelled at me to shut up and lie still.

Afterward, Chuck came in and kissed me, just like before. But it was not the tender moment it had been the first time. I started asking myself, "What am I doing here? How could I love this man who would let me go through this twice? I must be crazy!"

Chuck drove me home for the last time. I had submitted my resignation two weeks prior and would start a new job the next week. But something went wrong—I could not even get out of bed. I began to hemorrhage. I was weak and lost five pounds in forty-eight hours. I scarcely weighed ninety pounds and my friends said I looked like a skeleton. At the time I thought to myself, "That's just what I feel like—a skeleton. Dead to the world."

On New Year's Eve, two days after the abortion, I thought I was dying. I made my New Year's resolution right then. "If I come out of this alive, I will never even look at another man. They are all the same, self-centered and self-serving. I don't need anyone. I can do it all by myself."

I thought of Bob, and I thought of Chuck and my anger burned. I hated as I had never hated before. I hurt too. I felt used, abused, discarded, and worthless. I stayed stoned practically twenty-four-hours a day. There was a constant nagging in my soul that I could not identify. But I decided to pull myself up by the bootstraps and get on with life. I quit the drugs and would not allow myself to cry anymore. I hardened my heart so that no one would ever hurt me again.

I waited patiently for the Lord;
he turned to me and heard my cry.
He lifted me out of the slimy pit,
out of the mud and mire;
he set my feet on a rock
and gave me a firm place to stand.
He put a new song in my mouth,
a hymn of praise to our God.

(Ps. 40:1-3)

a healing place

Have you ever told your story?

Tell it now, to God and to yourself. Use the space here to begin, or start a separate, more private journal.

CHAPTER 2

just what is post-abortion syndrome?

A voice is heard in Ramah,
mourning and great weeping,
Rachel weeping for her children and
refusing to be comforted,
because her children are no more.

(Jer. 31:15)

"A woman doesn't want an abortion like she wants an ice-cream cone or a Porsche, but like an animal caught in a trap who gnaws off its own leg," Frederica Matthewes-Green, a pro-life feminist who started "Feminists for Life" has said.[1]

If you have had an abortion, you know exactly what she means. Abortion is not a procedure most women undergo casually. It is something you are driven to in desperation, when the alternatives seem too awful to contemplate. Yet, ironically, the very act meant to produce relief, in the long run, often produces its own special brand of agony.

In this sense, too, the quote hits home. Though the initial physical pain recedes, the emotional pain of abortion lingers like the phantom pain of an amputated limb. To our hearts, this deep, disturbing sense of unrest and regret is what is meant by the term Post-Abortion Syndrome. And that may be all the definition you need.

There is, however, a more technical description available. According to Dr. Vincent Rue, a psychotherapist who has researched the effects of abortion on post-abortive women for approximately twenty years, the term Post-Abortion Syndrome, or PAS, refers to a type of Post Traumatic Stress Disorder (PTSD) that is characterized by the chronic or delayed development of symptoms resulting from impacted emotional reactions to the perceived physical and emotional trauma of abortion. In other words, long after the abortion you may develop an emotional or physical reaction; others may have chronic, continuing reactions to the abortion. He proposes four symptoms of PAS: (1) exposure to or participation in an abortion experience, i.e., the intentional destruction of one's unborn child, which is perceived as traumatic and beyond the range of usual human experience; (2) uncontrolled negative reexperiencing of the abortion death event, e.g., flashbacks, nightmares, grief, and anniversary reactions; (3) unsuccessful attempts to avoid or deny abortion recollections and emotional pain, which result in reduced responsiveness to others and one's environment; and (4) experiencing associated symptoms not present before the abortion, including guilt about surviving.[2]

This leaves the woman with an inability to:

(1) process the fear, anger, sadness, and guilt surrounding her abortion experience
(2) grieve the loss of her baby, and
(3) come to peace with God, herself, and others involved in the abortion decision

Why do so many women experience PAS? After all, most women sincerely believed they were making the best decision they could at the time. Yet, even though abortion is legal, many women feel they have violated their own moral code by choosing it. There may be immediate relief, but any moral struggle felt prior to the abortion will resurface eventually. Even a woman who had no qualms about abortion at the time may later change her thinking about the issue, perhaps through learning more about fetal development, and come to regard with horror the choice she has made. Perhaps, too, a woman may find herself unable to conceive again, and experience profound regret at her lost opportunity for motherhood.

Unable to go back and "undo" the abortion, the post-abortive woman struggles to cope with the uncomfortable or frightening thoughts and feelings that sometimes plague her. She may try to rationalize her abortion, reminding herself over and over of why she chose it. She may even claim out loud to be glad for what she did, in hopes that if she says it loudly enough and often enough, she may come to believe it inside. She may try to block out the whole experience, pushing it completely out of her memory, or at least down so far that she doesn't need to think about it. Or she may try to make up for the abortion, perhaps working in the pro-life movement, becoming "Super Mom" to her other kids, or having an "atonement baby" soon after the abortion. If she had the abortion for a specific reason, like finishing college or saving a relationship, she may work extremely hard to make that reason valid in retrospect—i.e., becoming heavily invested in making her career a great success, or marrying the person she was afraid to go against, despite reservations.

These defense mechanisms are very effective in keeping the painful memories at bay, but they consume a lot of mental energy as a woman works to ignore powerful emotions. Eventually, if enough stress enters her life, she may find that she lacks the stamina to cope with both the current stresses and the past ones. During this time, almost anything—pictures of prenatal development, a new pregnancy, or even the whine of a dentist's drill that resembles the sound of the abortionist's equipment—may cause the symptoms of PAS to flare up, often causing her to wonder what in the world is going wrong. The symptoms of PAS will not necessarily appear at the same time, nor is any woman likely to experience the entire list. Some may occur immediately after an abortion, and others much later. However, if three or more of the symptoms listed below describe what you have been going through recently, chances are you are experiencing PAS.[3]

(1) **Guilt.** Guilt is what an individual feels when she has violated her own moral code. For the woman who has come to believe, at some point either before or after the abortion, that she consented to the killing of her unborn child, the burden of guilt is relentless. There is little consolation to offer the woman who has transgressed one of nature's strongest instincts: the protection a mother extends to her young. In fact, many post-abortive women believe that any unhappy events that have occurred since the abortion were inevitable because they "deserve it."

(2) **Anxiety.** Anxiety is defined as an unpleasant emotional and physical state of apprehension which may take the form of tension (inability to relax, irritability), physical responses (dizziness, pounding heart, upset stomach, headaches), worry about the future, difficulty concentrating, and disturbed sleep. The conflict between a woman's moral standards and her decision to abort generates much of this anxiety. Very often, she will not relate her anxiety to a past abortion, and yet she will unconsciously begin to avoid anything having to do with babies. She may make excuses for not attending a baby shower, skip the baby aisle at the grocery store, and so forth.

(3) **Psychological "numbing."** Many post-abortive woman maintain a secret vow that they will never again allow themselves to be put in such a vulnerable position. As a result, often without conscious thought, they may work hard to keep their emotions in tight check, preventing themselves from feeling the pain of what has happened, but also greatly hampering their ability to form and maintain close relationships. Cut off even from themselves, they may feel as though their lives were happening to another person.

(4) **Depression and thoughts of suicide.** All of us experience depression from time to time, but the following forms of it are certainly common in women who have experienced abortion:

- *Sad mood*—ranging from feelings of melancholy to total hopelessness.
- *Sudden and uncontrollable crying episodes*—the source of which appear to be a total mystery.
- *Deterioration of self-concept*—because she feels wholly deficient in her ability to function as a "normal" woman.
- *Sleep, appetite, and sexual disturbances*—usually in a pattern of insomnia, loss of appetite and/or reduced sex drive.
- *Reduced motivation*—for the normal activities of life. The things that occupied her life before the depression no longer seem worth doing.
- *Disruption in interpersonal relationships*—because of a general lack of enthusiasm for all activities. This is especially evidenced in her relationship with her husband or boyfriend, particularly if he was involved in the abortion decision.
- *Thoughts of suicide*—or preoccupation with death. Not surprisingly, in a study done by the Elliot Institute some 33 percent of post-abortive women surveyed reached a level of depression so deep that they would rather die than go on.[4] If you, or someone you know, has verbalized feelings this desperate, you

or they are experiencing the severest form of clinical depression. Please get immediate professional attention.

(5) **Anniversary syndrome.** In the same survey, some 54 percent of post-abortive women report an increase of PAS symptoms around the anniversary of the abortion and/or the due date of the aborted child.

(6) **Re-experiencing the abortion.** A very common event described by post-abortive women is the sudden distressing, recurring flashbacks of the abortion episode. Flashbacks often occur during situations that resemble some aspect of the abortion, such as a routine gynecological exam, or even the sound of a vacuum cleaner's suction. Flashbacks also occur in the form of recurring nightmares about babies in general or the aborted baby in particular. These dreams usually involve themes of lost, dismembered or crying babies.

(7) **Preoccupation with becoming pregnant again.** A significant percentage of women who abort become pregnant again within one year, and many others verbalize the desire to conceive again as quickly as possible. The new baby, sometimes referred to as the "atonement baby," may represent an unconscious desire to replace the one that was aborted.

(8) **Anxiety over fertility and childbearing issues.** Some post-abortive women maintain a fear that they will never again become pregnant or never be able to carry a pregnancy to term. Some expect to have handicapped children because they have "disqualified themselves as good mothers." Many refer to these fears as punishments from God.

(9) **Interruption of the bonding process with present and/or future children.** Fearing another devastating loss, a post-abortive

woman may not allow herself to truly bond with other children. Another common reaction is to atone for her actions toward the aborted child by becoming the world's most perfect mother to her remaining or future children. Likewise, the woman who already had children at the time of her abortion may discover that she is beginning to view them in a different light. At one extreme she may unconsciously devalue them, thinking things like, "You were the lucky ones. You were allowed to live." Or she may go in the opposite direction and become overly protective.

(10) **Survival guilt.** Most women do not abort for trivial reasons. They are usually in the midst of a heartbreaking situation where they stand to lose much if they choose to carry their pregnancies to term. In the end, the decision boils down to a sorrowful "it's me or you, and I choose me." But while the abortion frees them from their current trauma, it frequently produces in them an unrelenting guilt for choosing their own comfort over the life of the child.

(11) **Development of eating disorders.** Some post-abortive women developed anorexia or bulimia. While this phenomenon remains largely unexplored at this time, several factors may contribute to it. First, a substantial weight gain or severe weight loss is associated with unattractiveness, which reduces the odds of becoming pregnant again. Second, becoming unattractive serves as a form of self-punishment and helps perpetuate the belief that the woman is unworthy of anyone's attention. Third, extremes in eating behavior represent a form of control for the woman who feels her life is totally out of control. And finally, a drastic weight loss can shut down the menstrual cycle, thus preventing any future pregnancies.

(12) **Alcohol and drug abuse.** Alcohol and drug use often serve initially as a form of self-medication—a way of coping with the pain of the abortion memories. Sadly, the woman who resorts to alcohol

and/or drugs eventually finds herself having not only more problems but also fewer resources with which to solve them. The mental and physical consequences of alcohol or drug abuse only amplify most of the symptoms the woman is already experiencing.

(13) **Other self-punishing or self-degrading behaviors.** In addition to eating disorders and substance abuse, the post-abortive woman may also enter into abusive relationships, become promiscuous, fail to take care of herself medically, or deliberately hurt herself emotionally and/or physically.

(14) **Brief reactive psychosis.** Rarely, a post-abortive woman may experience a brief psychotic episode for two weeks or less after her abortion. The break with reality and subsequent recovery are both extremely rapid, and in most cases the person returns completely to normal when it is over. While this is an unusual reaction to abortion, it bears mentioning only because it is possible for a person to have a brief psychotic reaction to a stressful event without being labeled a psychotic individual. During such an episode, the individual's perception of reality is drastically distorted.

This book is written with the desire to assist those who have experienced abortion in understanding their feelings and gently urge them to work through the various stages of grieving. Won't you walk with us through the following steps and become free from the grief that grips your soul? If you will, you can put that list of symptoms behind you forever.

Have mercy on me, O God, have mercy on me,
for in you my soul takes refuge.
I will take refuge in the shadow of your wings
until the disaster has passed.
I cry out to God Most High,
to God, who fulfills his purpose for me.
He sends from heaven and saves me,
rebuking those who hotly pursue me;
God sends his love and faithfulness.

(Ps. 57:1-3)

a healing place

Think about your life. Are you experiencing any of the symptoms of Post-Abortion Syndrome? Using the list of symptoms in this chapter, identify those that could be a result of your abortion. Perhaps listing them here or in your journal will be the first step in putting them behind you.

CHAPTER 3

a wall of denial

I will give you a new heart and put a new spirit in you;
I will remove from you your heart of stone and give you
a heart of flesh.

(Ezek. 36:26)

It was done. Where before I had felt turmoil and anxiety, now I felt nothing. I was numb. And what was more, I no longer felt terrified of Bob. I was indifferent to what he thought or did because I didn't care anymore. About anything.

—Joan

Feelings of relief are common immediately after an abortion. You are free of the burden of an unplanned pregnancy, free from anxiety, free from the pressures related to the decision. Free! It's over. Life can return to normal . . . that is, as long as you can believe you did nothing wrong. Or as long as you can keep from thinking about it. According to Dr. Vincent Rue, President of the Institute for Pregnancy Loss, the great amounts of energy expended to keep the memories at bay are central to the development of post-abortion syndrome.[1]

Denial is a wall of protection that a woman puts up in order to cope with the reality of her decision. But it is not a difficult wall to erect. Society provides bricks, mortar, and even laborers for the job.

The wall was started during the decision-making process, raised a few bricks at a time, as we began to emotionally detach from the painful prospect of losing a part of ourselves. A huge section was raised during the abortion itself, and many bricks have been added over the years to make the wall taller and stronger. This wall is the buffer zone of denial to keep us safe from the horrible memories of losing our children and our own guilt in ending their lives.

Unfortunately, the same wall that keeps grief from our heart's door also keeps us separated from God's redeeming love. It has been raised to prevent pain and sorrow, but it also acts as a buffer to other emotions, such as joy and happiness. It may keep us safe, but it keeps us in prison, too.

C.S. Lewis said, "To love at all is to be vulnerable. Love anything, and your heart will certainly be wrung and possibly be broken. If you want to make sure of keeping it intact, you must give your heart to no one. . . . Wrap it carefully round with hobbies and little luxuries; avoid all entanglements; lock it up safe in the casket or coffin of your selfishness. But in that casket—safe, dark, motionless, airless—it will change. It will not be broken; it will become unbreakable, impenetrable, irredeemable."[2]

Only by opening the door of this wall to your heart and expressing your sorrow over this loss can healing begin. But before you can begin to break it down, you need to understand the ways in which you fortify it every day.

Denial under Construction

Two of the bricks, misinformation and the omission of information can lead a woman to believe the decision to abort is, physically, a safe one. One Planned Parenthood newsletter actually tried to convince the public that surgical abortion is safer to the mother than having a baby:

> Having an abortion is safer now than ever. Since the abortion procedure has been legalized and is now monitored, it is safer than giving birth or even getting a shot of penicillin, nor is it threatening to future fertility.[3]

Yet medical evidence is to the contrary. The reality is that abortion, like any surgical procedure, brings many risks, not only at the time of surgery, but also to future pregnancies. In his book *Lime 5*, Mark Crutcher, president of Life Dynamics, describes injury after injury caused by abortion. At the time his book was written he was currently providing litigation support in eighty-four malpractice cases, including eleven cases involving abortion-related deaths in the U.S.[4]

The "counseling" that many women receive before undergoing an abortion is full of euphemistic terms like "blob of tissue" and "termination of pregnancy." The woman is generally reassured of the legality of abortion, the inference being that anything legal must be okay. She is also comforted with such phrases as, "This is the best possible solution for you" and "A child would only complicate your life, maybe even ruin it. Think about the opportunities you would miss." Rarely in pro-abortion settings is a woman counseled that she is killing her child; the very thought would send a woman running. Neither is a woman urged to think of anyone but herself, except in such false ways as considering the kind of life the child would have if he were rejected by his father. The multitude of childless couples longing to adopt are not mentioned.

This dehumanizing of the baby only fosters the kind of denial that later comes to haunt most women who choose abortion.

Related Bricks

Three more bricks that post-abortive women generally have in abundant supply are guilt, shame, and anxiety. Let's look at each of these up close and see whether they form any part of your wall.

Guilt

We hear a lot about guilt these days. We're reassured over and over of God's forgiveness and encouraged to give ourselves room to fail. This is all well and good. Feelings of guilt that occur when you've done nothing wrong, or that linger after forgiveness has been granted—these are false guilt, and they should be put aside.

But true guilt is another matter. When you have broken one of God's laws, true guilt results. While we may not have looked at our abortion as a sin at the time, it was one just the same. God makes it very clear in Scripture that He is the author of all life:

> I praise you because I am fearfully and wonderfully made;
> your works are wonderful,
> I know that full well.
> My frame was not hidden from you
> when I was made in the secret place.
> When I was woven together in the depths of the earth,
> your eyes saw my unformed body.
> All the days ordained for me
> were written in your book
> before one of them came to be (Ps. 139:14-16).

We played God's role by ending our children's lives in an effort to erase our mistake and hide it from the world. Guilty feelings probably played a role in your having an abortion in the first place . . . guilt over what a crisis pregnancy would do to your family, to your boyfriend, even to the baby itself. Yet the very act that was supposed to alleviate that guilt only produced guilt of a different sort—true guilt before God.

But there is wonderful news. You don't have to live with that guilt forever; it can be forgiven! 1 John 1:9 tells us: "If we confess our sins, he is faithful and just and will forgive us our sins and purify us from all unrighteousness."

God can remove the awful gnawing of that guilt from our souls, and what's more, He longs to do it! But the more you try to escape that guilt in other ways, the more bricks you add to your wall—and the more you seal yourself off from a thriving relationship with God, as well as from truly experiencing the joys that life has to offer.

One psalmist described the feelings of ignored guilt this way: "When I kept silent, my bones wasted away through my groaning all day long. For day and night your hand was heavy upon me; my strength was sapped" (Ps. 32:3-4).

If this describes the way you've been feeling, it may be because God is urging you to turn to Him. Sometimes the only way we will do this is for Him to make us feel so low that all we can do is to look up to Him.

The only way to receive relief from guilt is acknowledging your sins to God. Remember that God knows everything—including the truth about your abortion. Trust Him with your heart and let the wall fall down. You'll be amazed at the view on the other side, just as the psalmist was:

> Then I acknowledged my sin to you
> and did not cover up my iniquity.
> I said, "I will confess
> my transgressions to the Lord"—
> and you forgave
> the guilt of my sin (Ps. 32:5).

Shame

Another common brick in the post-abortive heart is shame. Satan continually whispers in our ears the lie that if anyone knew about this sin, they would hate us.

In an effort to protect yourself from this potential rejection, you may hide the abortion from those around you. Or you may go to the opposite extreme and tell everyone around you, driven by your hunger to have them answer the question: "Will you still love me if you know the truth?"

Satan has quite an arsenal of other poison arrows as well, which he hurls in your mind day and night:

Sometimes the thoughts of unworthiness flooded my mind until I thought I would scream. I kept hearing the words, "You're not worthy of anything good. You don't deserve forgiveness. How could you kill three babies? You deserve anything bad that happens to you, and worse." It was worse at night when I went to bed. I couldn't sleep for the thoughts that raced inside my head, leading from one scenario to another of doom and gloom. Instead of confiding in someone trustworthy about these battles that raged on in my head, I kept them locked up inside me, too ashamed to admit my struggle to anyone.

—Joan

The American Heritage Dictionary defines the word shame as "a painful emotion caused by a strong sense of guilt, embarrassment, unworthiness, or disgrace."[5] But any woman who has had an abortion doesn't need a dictionary to tell her about shame. She could write a dictionary on it herself.

Psalm 25:3 tells us that "no one whose hope is in [God] will ever be put to shame, but they will be put to shame who are treacherous without excuse." When you seek the Lord, confess your sins, and ask Him to forgive you, you are released from shame. Psalms 34:4-5 relays this truth:

I sought the Lord, and he answered me;
he delivered me from all my fears.

> Those who look to him are radiant;
> their faces are never covered with shame.

You will likely be pleasantly surprised at people's reactions to your long-held secret; the condemning few are mostly just on television. But no matter what anyone else thinks, once you confess your sin to God, your shame will evaporate. If you can hold your head up before God, you can do it before anyone.

Anxiety

Your wall doesn't have to crumble much before anxiety begins to pour in. Any thought of the aborted baby as a real child, and the questions will begin. Was it a boy or a girl? Who would she have looked like? What would we be doing now if I had kept her? Seeing a baby, or a little girl or boy who would be about the same age, triggers the anxiety. Is that what he'd look like? I wonder if her hair would have been like that? Every time one of those questions is asked you force yourself to set it aside. You can't allow yourself to think such thoughts because they are too painful.

You may never know the answers to these questions, and that unknowingness makes you vulnerable to anguish and despair. Each time you set these questions aside, you put off thinking about your child as a living human being and add another brick to your wall.

People in Denial

Denial is not new with the legalization of abortion. It's not even new to the twentieth century. In fact, the Bible is full of examples of people in denial—not just to God and others, but to themselves.

Eve's Story (Gen. 3:2-20)

Ironically, the first story about denial involves the very first woman—Eve, in the Garden of Eden. It's a familiar tale. Adam and Eve are given the run of the Garden, except for one tree, which has been forbidden to them. Satan, disguised as a snake, tempts Eve to eat the fruit of that tree, and she succumbs, convincing Adam to go along. When confronted by God, she turns the blame onto the snake.

How many of us, after our abortions, began to support the pro-choice movement? Like Eve recruiting Adam, did we need company in our wrongdoing to make it feel acceptable? Finding acceptance can add a powerful brick to our wall of denial. And like Eve when God confronted her, how many of us blamed others for their bad advice or lack of support instead of assuming the responsibility for our own actions?

Just as Eve was deceived into believing that the forbidden fruit would make her smarter, many women today are deceived into believing that an unplanned pregnancy will ruin their lives. They are mistaken—just as Eve was.

David's Story (2 Sam. 11)

Even one of the heroes of the Bible, David, tried to hide from his sin—a sin, incidentally, much like ours.

Bathsheba, a lovely young woman, was bathing on a rooftop, and David caught sight of her. Quite naturally aroused, he decided to act on his desire, and he had her brought to him. The result of his passion was a pregnancy, his child conceived in the womb of another man's wife.

David first tried to cover up his actions by bringing her soldier-husband Uriah home from battle in the hopes that he would lie with her and then assume that the child was his own. When this plan didn't work, David had Uriah sent to the front lines, knowing he would be killed and that Bathsheba would then be free to marry David, thus legitimizing the pregnancy.

Deception, manipulation, even murder . . . all to avoid being found out. Was it any different with our abortions? In our panic we added more bricks to the wall. Weren't we willing to go to any lengths rather than face our friends or family members with the truth, risking rejection and judgment, possibly losing our reputation, our lifestyle, and the opportunities we've anticipated?

Peter's Story (Luke 22:54-62)

Imagine knowing Jesus as a flesh-and-blood human being. Imagine being selected as His special disciple, walking with Him by the Sea of Galilee, watching His miracles in amazement and listening in awe to His teachings. How could you experience Christ face-to-face and not be completely loyal to Him? Yet that's what happened to Peter.

One minute he was declaring his absolute loyalty to the Savior; the next, he was abandoning Him in His time of greatest need. The soldiers had taken Jesus away to be tried and crucified. Peter followed and was recognized as one of His friends. But when asked if he knew Jesus, he denied it on three occasions.

His denial, of course, stemmed from his fear of getting the same treatment Jesus was getting. But as Jesus predicted, when Peter heard the cock crow he realized he had denied the Lord three times, his wall of denial crumbled in a torrent of weeping as he begged for forgiveness.

Denial within You

Have you built a wall of denial? If so, try to reconstruct the process through which you convinced yourself that your abortion was a good decision. The following questions may help.

- What were your fears at the time of the abortion?
- What pressures did you experience, and from whom?

You may not even have recognized the wall of denial being built in your life. If you believed all the misinformation and lies that were told, then you may have thought it truly was a good choice for you at the time. But since it is a legitimate loss, your subconscience may have responded for you. You may not have understood the Post-Abortion Syndrome thoughts and behaviors at the time, but you are just beginning to understand them now.

- What was your understanding of abortion, and how did you gain this understanding?

In her Bible study titled *Forgiven and Set Free Bible Study,* Linda Cochrane lists some of the arguments commonly used to build and keep the wall of denial firmly in place. Do some of them represent the bricks in your own wall?

I just terminated a pregnancy; I didn't kill a baby.

Abortion is legal, so how can it be wrong?

Everyone must decide for themselves when life begins.

It happened so long ago; why bring it up now?

Everyone around me said it would be the best thing to do.

Jesus has said that the truth, His truth, will make us free (John 8:32) and part of that encompasses freedom from denial, living a lie. Just as we have built our walls of denial brick by brick, we must begin the work of tearing them down brick by brick with the truth. Are you ready to begin the work? If so, take a quiet moment to tear down the lies and replace them with the truth.

I just terminated a pregnancy; I didn't kill a baby.

For you created my inmost being;
you knit me together in my mother's womb.
I praise you because I am fearfully and wonderfully made;
your works are wonderful,
I know that full well.
My frame was not hidden from you
when I was made in the secret place.

> When I was woven together in the depths of the earth,
> your eyes saw my unformed body.
> All the days ordained for me
> were written in your book
> before one of them came to be (Ps. 139:13-16).

Abortion is legal, so how can it be wrong?

> There is a way that seems right to a man, but in the end it leads to death (Prov. 14:12).

Everyone must decide for themselves when life begins.

> Where is the wise man? Where is the scholar? Where is the philosopher of this age? Has not God made foolish the wisdom of the world? (1 Cor. 1:20; see also Ps. 139:13-16).

It happened so long ago; why bring it up now?

> Nothing in all creation is hidden from God's sight. Everything is uncovered and laid bare before the eyes of him to whom we must give account (Heb. 4:13).

Everyone around me said it would be the best thing to do.

> Am I now trying to win the approval of men, or of God? Or am I trying to please men? If I were still trying to please men, I would not be a servant of Christ (Gal. 1:10).[6]

In his testimony before a congressional committee, Dr. C. Everett Koop said, "The consequences to the fetus [in abortion] are undeniable."[7] In your heart, you know this; that's why you picked up this book. But what the heart knows, the mind sometimes has trouble accepting. Yet before you can begin to heal, you will have to acknowledge consciously the truth of what you have done—that your decision to abort ended the life of your unborn child.

How can you begin to tear down your wall of denial? Facing the truth that abortion ended a life is the first step in grieving, allowing the woman to understand that her emotions following her abortion are in response to her losing a child.

Linda Cochrane also suggests answering these questions in order to tear down a few more bricks:

I had an abortion to relieve the pressure of . . .

I had an abortion because I was afraid others around me would think . . .

I could no longer deny my loss when . . .[8]

This last question presents a turning point.

For me it was when I was having an ultrasound on my oldest son, Bruce, at about sixteen weeks. I expected to see a blob of tissue. When the screen revealed my fully formed son—complete with ten fingers and ten toes, I knew the truth. I hadn't aborted a blob of tissue—but a baby.

—Sydna

For you, that moment may not yet have come. Perhaps now is the time to take out all the memories you have worked so hard to suppress, open the door to that closet in your mind where those dark scrapbooks are hidden.

It's time to clean house. But it won't be easy. Facing our mistakes never is, and this one is likely to bring a depth of grief and regret unparalleled so far in your life. It would be a good idea to join a support group as you go through this, or at least confide in a supportive friend. However, in releasing the denial, you will find once again a measure of relief. For in acknowledging the truth, you will be giving yourself the opportunity to grieve consciously what you have been grieving subconsciously all along—the death of your own child.

God's Response to Your Abortion

One of the hardest things about bringing your sin into the light is the realization that, not only can you see it, but God can too. It may be comforting to remember that, to Him, your abortion has never been hidden. He knew your baby before you even knew of his or her existence. He has always known the circumstances of his or her conception. He was with them as they were being formed in your womb, and He was present when your baby died. *And He is with your child even now.*

As He is with you. And as He was with Eve, and with David, and with Peter.

He knew of all your turmoil way back then. He knew what you thought. He knew what you had been told, what pressures you were under, what fears you faced, and what cowardices or temptations won you over. He loved you then, and He still loves you now.

Take heart from these words of Paul's:

> I thank Christ Jesus our Lord, who has given me strength, that he considered me faithful, appointing me to his service. Even though I was once a blasphemer and a persecutor and a violent man, I was shown mercy because I acted in ignorance and unbelief. The grace of our Lord was poured out on me abundantly, along with the faith and love that are in Christ Jesus. Here is a trustworthy saying that deserves full acceptance: Christ Jesus came into the world to save sinners—of whom I am the worst. But for that very reason I was shown mercy so that in me, the worst of sinners, Christ Jesus might display his unlimited patience as an example for those who would believe on him and receive eternal life (1Tim. 1:12-16).

You mustered up the courage to enter the abortion clinic that day; now summon that courage back again, this time to call on the

Lord. He can free you from the guilt of this sin. Stop now and ask Him to reveal to you the things your mind has hidden from conscious thought since the abortion. Remembering is the first step in tearing down the wall of denial. Trust that He will not burden you with more than your heart can bear. It's a painful step, but it is the first one on the road to real relief . . . a relief that will last. Please read on, and we'll walk with you through each of the emotions that may flood your soul.

> *I signed up to volunteer at the crisis pregnancy center. The only requirements were to know Jesus as Savior and to have a servant's heart. I went to the training class. There it was in black and white. Fetal development. The heart begins beating at 18 to 21 days. By six weeks the central nervous system is in place. They can feel stimuli. I thought, "Oh dear God, what have I done?" I could look no one at the training class in the eye. The walls were closing in around me. I had to get out! I had to escape!*
>
> —Joan

Create in me a pure heart, O God,
and renew a steadfast spirit within me.
Do not cast me from your presence
or take your Holy Spirit from me.
Restore to me the joy of your salvation
and grant me a willing spirit, to sustain me.
Then I will teach transgressors your ways,
and sinners will turn back to you.
Save me from bloodguilt, O God,
the God who saves me,
and my tongue will sing of your righteousness.
O Lord, open my lips,
and my mouth will declare your praise . . .
The sacrifices of God are a broken spirit;
a broken and contrite heart,
O God, you will not despise.

(Ps. 51:10-17)

a healing place

Perhaps you've been denying the truth about your abortion. Just as the wall of denial is built slowly, the wall will probably come down slowly. It may take days . . . weeks . . . and even months. You'll think the wall is gone, and you'll find another pile of bricks. Give yourself time to dismantle the wall of denial.

Record your cries to God here or in your journal, asking Him to reveal those hidden things. Then, as they are revealed, it may be helpful to write them down as a way to release them to God.

CHAPTER 4

bitter roots: anger

. . . that no bitter root grows up to cause trouble
and defile many.

(Heb. 12:15)

Suppressed anger brewed under the surface of my emotions, causing the roots of bitterness to grow deep in my heart. I hated the men involved in my abortions. I was angry at God. After all, He could have stopped me. Mostly I was angry at myself. My lack of information and ignorance was inexcusable. Hatred seemed to consume my life as my anger was way out of control. Unfortunately it was those closest to me who suffered from the outbursts, depression, and drug abuse.

—Joan

> Emotions play a pivotal role in the event of a crisis. They become the avenue by which we vent our feelings of anger and pain, sadness and remorse. When we don't allow those emotions to play their important role in the process of healing at the time of the event, they will resurface in the future.[1]

One of the strongest of human passions, anger, seldom leaves us without being addressed directly. When denied, it finds other ways to express itself, often through bitterness or depression. Yet when it is expressed inappropriately, it can be terribly destructive to anyone unfortunate enough to be in its path.

Signs of "aftershock," a word coined by Dr. Andrew Scaby to describe any significant delayed response to a crisis,[2] may vary from sleep disturbances, jumpiness, nightmares, guilt and numbness.

> *I experienced all the above-stated symptoms. My sleep was constantly interrupted by dreams involving delivering dead babies. The numbness that had protected me from the initial pain of my experience became the tool that chiseled away at the softness of my heart, leaving me hard and indifferent to life.*
>
> —Joan

Dr. Anne C. Speckhard, in a survey of post-abortive women, found that 92 percent of those surveyed reported feelings of anger related to their abortions, and most of them expressed surprise at the intensity of those feelings.[3] Unsure how to handle it, many worked hard to keep it in check, succeeding only in driving it underground to seethe and fester and express itself in other ways. Many women find themselves having spontaneous, emotional outbursts triggered by the least provocation. They can't seem to control their emotions or figure out where they are coming from, which is as confusing for the individual as it is to those closest to her.

Whether it seethes on the surface or hides underneath, anger is an emotion that needs attention. When it's related to abortion, it often acts as a roadblock to healing—around which there is no detour. The good news is that it's an emotion familiar to our heavenly Father. And with His help we can find a healthy way of handling it.

Anger in the Bible

We tend to think of anger as a negative quality, something that demands our repentance. Yet it's a quality God Himself bestowed upon humanity. In fact, it's a quality He possesses.

God's Anger

It's not hard at all to find biblical examples of God getting angry. Old Testament pages flow with it! Psalm 78:49-50 gives a graphic description of His attitude toward the Egyptians, who had enslaved the Israelites: "He unleashed against them his hot anger, his wrath, indignation and hostility—a band of destroying angels. He prepared a path for his anger . . . "

In Genesis 19:1-20 the story of God's anger against Sodom and Gomorrah is a familiar one. Because of the wickedness of the people of Sodom, God rained fire and brimstone upon the entire city, killing all who lived there. A quick glance through a concordance gives us many more instances when God's wrath was displayed.

Not only does God allow anger, He encourages it—when it's directed against evil. Much of the anger related to your abortion undoubtedly qualifies.

Jesus' Anger

Few who have ever attended Sunday School could have missed the story of Jesus' anger toward the moneychangers in the temple. Like Father, like Son—He was outraged to have this holy place used like a common flea market, for selfish profit, distracting those who had come to worship. John 2:13-16 relates the story:

> When it was almost time for the Jewish Passover, Jesus went up to Jerusalem. In the temple courts he found men selling cattle, sheep and doves, and others sitting at tables exchanging money. So he made a whip out of cords, and drove all from the temple area, both sheep and cattle; he scattered the coins of the money changers and overturned their tables. To those who sold doves he said, "Get these out of here! How dare you turn my Father's house into a market!"

Hardly a calm reaction! There's not a thing wrong with anger itself, even intense anger; in fact, there's a lot right with it.

Anger in Us

We know from experience, however, that anger can be used destructively, hurting both people and relationships. There are two ways in which it can be misused. First, it can be misused when it arises from selfish indignation rather than righteous indignation. For instance, Jesus' anger toward the moneychangers was righteous—they were behaving inappropriately in a place of worship. Now, had he been angry because He had planned on selling doves as well and they had cheated Him out of the best location . . . that would have been anger for nothing but self-serving purposes.

The second way anger can be misused is in its expression. Notice that Jesus drove out the right people, the moneychangers. He addressed their behavior, not their beings. How often have we found ourselves exploding at our children's beings for leaving their beds unmade or clothes on the floor, when the real source of our anger is something else entirely? And how many times, when hurt or offended, have we found ourselves calling people names and hurling insults? These are the times when the expression of our anger crosses the line into sin's territory.

Digging Up the Bitter Roots

Have you driven angry feelings so far down inside that they have sprung up as plants with different names, like depression or despair, or perhaps self-destructive behaviors? It's critical that you dig out those tough roots. They are like weeds in your garden: persistent, pervasive, and fully capable of choking out any good seeds you may plant there. You may need to do some emotional probing to find out the true source of those feelings. Ask God to help you see any areas of bitterness or resentment that have remained in your heart. The following list of common targets of post-abortive anger may help:

- People who withheld the truth about the procedure.
- Friends who urged abortion as the best option.
- Self, for being in the situation to begin with, and for not having enough courage to go through with the pregnancy.
- Self for not educating yourself about fetal development and abortion techniques.
- The father of the baby, for not being supportive, whether physically, emotionally, or financially.
- Parents, for pressuring the situation or even insisting upon your abortion.
- God for allowing the pregnancy to happen or for not intervening to stop the abortion.

Once you've identified the source—or more likely, sources—of your anger, you'll notice that some of them will be legitimate and others will not. However, there is still a need for these emotions to be expressed in some way to relieve the bitterness in your heart. Emotions are not always rational, but our responses to them certainly can be.

Begin by praying that God would direct you in how to address your angry feelings. Most of them can probably be dealt with in the privacy of your own heart, but there may be some that will necessitate your talking to another person. Be slow to do that. Remember, you are uncovering hurts that had scabbed over long ago. To you, the words may feel new and raw all over again, and it may take some time to gain perspective on them.

A good way to begin is to write letters that you never intend to mail. Pour out all your feelings of rage, betrayal, hurt, or disillusionment onto paper. If they need further expression, do it with a trusted, but uninvolved, friend or counselor. As time eases the intensity, you will know whether or not to address the issues with the people who were involved in the abortion decision.

Bear in mind that God, Himself, will take vengeance on those who have hurt you, if it is necessary. Romans 12:19 says: "Do not take revenge, my friends, but leave room for God's wrath, for it is written: 'It is mine to avenge; I will repay,' says the Lord."

I had killed three babies! Once I acknowledged that fact, my anger toward those involved in my abortions was intense. I thought of Bob and Chuck and my anger burned. How could they have put me in that position? I thought of those professionals who performed the abortions and I fumed. How could they have lied to me? Why didn't they tell me the truth about fetal development? I began with the doctor, pouring out my rage on paper, detailing every point of my fury, addressing him by name. Then I wrote to Bob and then Chuck. Letter after letter I wrote, until I had exhausted every person and every reason for anger my heart could dredge up. It took time and energy to uncover the depth of emotion I had toward so many people. But letter by letter, person by person, the anger seemed to subside. Though never mailed, the result of the letters was a heavy burden released and, finally peace.[4]

—Joan

Do not fret because of evil men
or be envious of those who do wrong;
for like the grass they will soon wither,
like green plants they will soon die away.
Trust in the Lord and do good;
dwell in the land and enjoy safe pasture.
Delight yourself in the Lord
and he will give you the desires of your heart.
Commit your way to the Lord;
trust in him and he will do this:
He will make your righteousness shine like the dawn,
the justice of your cause like the noonday sun.
Be still before the Lord and wait patiently for him;
do not fret when men succeed in their ways,
when they carry out their wicked schemes.
Refrain from anger and turn from wrath;
do not fret—it leads only to evil.

(Ps. 37:1-8)

a healing place

Anger that is allowed to take root in our hearts grows deep roots of bitterness. Pause now to begin probing your angry feelings. Ask God to help you identify who and what you're angry about. Then begin writing those letters you'll never send. Perhaps you'll write one, or more, now. Perhaps days or weeks from now you'll want to write more.

Don't expect the release of anger to come all at once. Give yourself time to pray, reflect, and release the anger. The healing will come in time.

CHAPTER 5

a river of tears: grieving your loss

The hearts of the people cry out to the Lord.
O wall of the Daughter of Zion,
let your tears flow like a river day and night;
give yourself no relief, your eyes no rest.
Arise, cry out in the night, as the watches of the night begin;
pour out your heart like water in the presence of the Lord.
Lift up your hands to him for the lives of your children . . .

(Lam. 2:18-19)

I remember being alone in my dorm room seven months after the abortion . . . near the time that I should have been giving birth. I refused to think about it, but my body's own time clock was signaling the truth.

A friend—not even a close friend—had betrayed me that week. I found myself crying as though I'd never stop. All night long I cried, until my eyes were swollen shut. I even considered suicide, and I made up my mind never to trust anyone again. It was obviously an over-reaction, but it would be years before I could acknowledge the true source of my pain that night. I was subconsciously grieving the death of my unborn child during the week he would have been born.

—Sydna

It is terrifying for many to consider actually mourning the loss of their aborted children. Tears of remorse are difficult to release because we fear that these emotions will consume us. The looming presence of this pain may drive us to great fear. Thoughts of suicide may creep in and out of our mind because it sounds easier than touching that pain. Often we ignore it or deny it.

But God has not forgotten us. We are as visible to Him as we were before the abortion. To use the analogy of a wall again, He will help us knock down that wall, brick by brick. He will be there to help us clear away the rubble that is left. What we fear is the pain of the truth, our guilt and shame. What He knows is that the darkness of this wall blocks the light of His mercy and grace.

It is not until you acknowledge your baby as a lost child that you will be able to grieve his or her loss. If you were to lose a baby after a live birth, or if you were to miscarry a child you wanted, you would expect to grieve, and deeply. And in the process of mourning, you would begin to heal.

The thought of grieving a baby that you chose to abort in the first place seems so contrary. You may have been told that since it wasn't really a baby to begin with, there is nothing to grieve—so you have resisted those feelings.

Yet even though this baby was lost by choice, you have nevertheless lost a child. Your heart still needs to grieve. It is that grief that will break down the wall. You needn't be afraid of the pain. God will walk through it with you. Though you may cry for days yet to come, remember:

> Those who sow in tears
>   will reap with songs of joy.
> He who goes out weeping,
>   carrying seed to sow,
> Will return with songs of joy,
>   carrying sheaves with him (Ps. 126:5-6).

Remember when David committed adultery with Bathsheba, then had Uriah killed? When the child died, David comforted Bathsheba who was grieving. And when Lazarus died and was in the tomb, Jesus, even knowing full well that He was about to restore life, showed us how to mourn the loss of someone we love. The Bible very simply says, "Jesus wept." (John 11:35) It is okay to cry, to weep great tears of sorrow over the loss of a loved one. That is how we can release the pent-up grief, how we can mourn our loss.

God developed the concept of mourning to allow us a way to release the pain of loss. It is a human trait to need closure after the death of a loved one. Funerals and wakes are all "passage" rituals that ensure mourning and encourage tears.

Sometimes the process is quick. But usually, the destruction of the wall around our hearts takes months or even years. Maybe the pain is too great to deal with all at once, or maybe we resist the process. You may take down a load of bricks only to mortar half of them back in place again. But be patient. Enjoy the rays of sun that will sometimes stream through the cracks. And when the grief threatens to overwhelm you, look forward to the days that are promised in Isaiah 60:20: " . . . the Lord will be your everlasting light, and your days of sorrow will end."

What an incredible promise! How wonderful to know that your days of sorrow will end! The thing that you've been so afraid of will be behind you forever. Never again will you live in darkness or fear. The wall will no longer be necessary because God's love has released you from your sin.

There it was in black and white. The booklet described the classic symptoms of post-abortion syndrome and I had them. Now I knew why the third week of March was always hard—it was the anniversary of my baby's due date. It took all my courage, but I dialed the number of the crisis pregnancy center and enrolled in a ten-week post-abortion counseling and education class. And the wall began to come down.

—Sydna

It's important to remember that God is no stranger to pain. His people experienced pain throughout the Old Testament. The Psalms, as well as the Book of Job, are filled with tears. Lamentations (which means "funeral songs") was most likely written by the Prophet Jeremiah, and he was grieving about the destruction of Jerusalem.

If the Lord created us in His own image, He created our tears as well, and He wants to use them to make us stronger. In being able to cry, you bring yourself humbly before the Lord. Pride is dissolved and the love you have stored in your heart is released. Tears indicate love for the child you lost so many years ago.

The First Step Toward Peace

Tears can be the first step toward peace in your heart over your abortion experience. Remember the passage in Luke 7 when Jesus was anointed by a sinful woman? While the passage doesn't reveal her name, it states that she had lived a sinful life. Verse 38 shares the story of how her tears endeared her to Jesus:

> As she stood behind him at his feet weeping, she began to wet his feet with her tears. Then she wiped them with her hair, kissed them and poured perfume on them.

Jesus' reaction to her tears was love and admiration. He informed the judgmental Pharisee in verse 47 that "her many sins have been forgiven—for she loved much." Later He spoke to her directly and said, "Your faith has saved you; go in peace."

Realize that your tears are precious and God wants to use them to ease your pain. This release means that the walls are coming down and His love can flow freely into your heart. Open up and give yourself permission to cry.

A Time to Mourn

The Bible is very clear that there are to be set times of mourning For example, listen to Ecclesiastes 3:1 and 4:

> There is a time for everything . . .
> a time to weep and a time to laugh,
> a time to mourn and a time to dance.

In biblical times, people wore sackcloth and ashes to inform the world of their emotions. While our society believes that you should swallow the pain and "get over it," God didn't make us that way. He designed our grieving times to be events which bring us closer to Him for comfort. Consider the words of Psalm 23:4: "Even though I walk through the valley of the shadow of death, I will fear no evil, for you are with me; your rod and your staff, they comfort me."

It is not uncommon for women going through post-abortion grief to cry for long periods of time. Sometimes you cry because of triggers—a song on the radio that reminds you of the abortion period in your life, seeing the father of your aborted child, meeting a child the same age your child would have been. While you may feel as though you are going crazy because you cannot predict your tears, realize that your reaction is normal.

When emotions have been bottled up inside for so many years, they can overcome you like an ocean wave hitting the beach. You don't know which way is up and you can't find a solid footing. But just as soon as the wave of emotions launches upon our hearts, it rolls back into the ocean leaving us feeling out of breath and trying to stabilize ourselves before the next wave hits.

The main thing to remember about grief is that you don't get over it—you get through it. Grief doesn't touch everyone the same way. Many women going through Bible studies in local crisis pregnancy centers watch others cry openly, yet remain completely calm and rational themselves. They have kept these emotions at bay for so many years that it takes exposure to the truth to break down their wall of composure. Maybe it isn't until a point of discussion blasts open a hole in their emotional wall that their true feelings finally hit them. At this point tears pour out for days on end. Then, all of a sudden, they are finished crying. Never judge another person's grieving methods. God made us all unique individuals for His own purposes.

Getting Through the Pain

You might be asking yourself—how long am I going to feel this pain? Will I ever be normal again? You will never be the same person you were before the abortion, but you can experience peace and healing in time. Give yourself permission to take as long as you need to grieve. If you need to walk slowly, painfully, deliberately through the center of your grief, go right ahead. But while you can lean on others, the work of getting through grief lies squarely on your own shoulders. Keep in mind that you are experiencing a normal reaction to death—even though your child died some time ago.

Each person must discover the coping skills that work best for her. Sometimes talking with a close friend, minister, or counselor and sharing your feelings about your lost child is comforting. Pets can also be therapeutic because they are non-judgmental companions whose only role is to love us. Many individuals find solace in reading psalms or books about how other people deal with grief.

Journaling is an excellent way to release emotions and bring you to greater understanding about your true feelings. It's common to write blindly and then reread your entries to find things about yourself that you didn't consciously realize before. In understanding your emotions, you can take the next step of coming to terms with them.

Again, writing letters you never intend to send is another way of expressing your feelings to people involved. Other activities that can help us cope include: cooking, physical exercise, reading, playing a musical instrument, gardening, housecleaning, shopping, or just going to work

When Others Don't Understand

You must remember that it is difficult for friends and family to understand the exact pain you are experiencing. Many husbands feel powerless to comfort their wives and suggest that they stop thinking about the abortion. Statements like, "Don't bring up all that junk now—it will only cause you pain," are common in households where women are grieving. What they don't realize is that you aren't dredging up the pain—it's with you always like a knot in your throat. You can no longer deny its existence. In order to get through the pain, you must experience these emotions.

Don't be angry if your husband, family, or friends can't understand what you are going through. While these feelings can totally engross you, others calmly go on with life. They laugh and talk about trivial things while you writhe in agony. This can make you angry and frustrated. You want to run away from them and scream, but you discover that no matter where you go, your grief follows you. You may need to find a private place to open your heart without others interfering with this step of the healing process.

Individuals may expect you not to grieve because it makes them uncomfortable. Maybe they have never had a loss, and they don't understand what you're feeling. In this circumstance you end up facing your grief alone. Try not to judge those who cannot help you. After your season of grief is over, gently relay how you were feeling to them in an effort to educate them

Post-abortive women can be the worst enemies of the mourning process. Keep in mind that if you share your grief to another PAS woman who is still in the denial stage of her emotions, she could easily discredit your feelings in order to fortify her own wall. Unless you discover someone who is truly at your point in the grieving process, try not to confide in other post-abortive individuals.

Children can be the most difficult group when it comes to understanding your feelings. Imagine if your mother started crying uncontrollably. Wouldn't you try to help her feel better any way you could? Your world revolves around this loved one and standing back while she is hurting is impossible. Remember that unless your children are adults, they simply cannot be burdened with this pain. Try to keep in control around young children. During a composed period, let them know that you are going through a hard time and that it has nothing to do with anything they have done. If restraint is impossible, ask a friend to baby-sit while you go out and have a good cry.

Should you come to a point in your healing process where you relay the truth about your abortion to your children, give them time to understand and express their emotions. Remember that they have also experienced a loss—even though they never knew this sibling. Their feelings need to be sorted out and you can help them when your tears are released.

Give yourself the next few weeks or months to experience every emotion that comes your way. Try not to take on a new job or make a big move, but relax and accept the emotions as they come. Be confident that your feelings are normal and that you are physically unable to deny them any longer. Ask family and friends to be patient with you—this is your season of grief. Understand that it won't last forever, but that on the other side of the pain, there is peace.

I will remember that day forever—March 28, 1989. It had been an anniversary week. I was led by two friends back to the "scene of the crime" to the first abortion. It was then that I remembered everything and reexperienced the abortion.

At long last the dam broke. Rivers of tears poured uncontrollably down my face. For the first time in seven years I was crying. Really crying! I could not stop myself. All the pain and heartache of those years was coming to the surface and overflowing. I was finally able to grieve for my children. I needed to mourn the loss. . . .

—Joan

I love you, O Lord, my strength.
The Lord is my rock, my fortress and my deliverer;
my God is my rock, in whom I take refuge.
He is my shield and the horn of my salvation, my stronghold.
I call to the Lord, who is worthy of praise,
and I am saved from my enemies.
The cords of death entangled me;
the torrents of destruction overwhelmed me.
The cords of the grave coiled around me;
the snares of death confronted me.
In my distress I called to the Lord;
I cried to my God for help.
From his temple he heard my voice;
my cry came before him, into his ears.

(Ps. 18:1-6)

a healing place

Are you ready to tear down a few more bricks from your wall? To mourn for your child? Spend time in prayer, using one of the psalms quoted in this chapter or your own words to pour out your thoughts, your anguish to God.

Record here or in your journal the slivers or rays of light you see as the wall disintegrates. Over the next few weeks and months, watch and record as the light increases in intensity.

CHAPTER 6

the heart of the matter: forgiveness

Bear with each other and forgive whatever
grievances you may have against one another.
Forgive as the Lord forgave you.

(Col. 3:13)

I was angry at my mother for being emotionally weak. If I had been able to confide in her, maybe my baby would still be alive. In my torn mind, she was responsible for my son's death even though she never knew I was pregnant.

—Sydna

Forgiveness. In all of Christianity, there is probably no concept more familiar; after all, our very salvation depends upon God's forgiveness of our sins. Yet, for all its familiarity, forgiveness is probably the aspect of Christianity people wrestle with most deeply. Some find it hard to believe God has really forgiven their sins. Others just can't forgive themselves. And we've all struggled with forgiving others.

If you've had an abortion, forgiveness is likely to be a word you can't hear without feeling as though a fist has been clinched around your heart. The issues surrounding that topic are probably numerous and conflicting. Simultaneously you may have emotions of guilt, resentment, bitterness, shame, anger, hopelessness . . . just to name a few. There is so much to sort out and seemingly no good way to go about it. It may seem easier just to jam those feelings back in, to not think about them.

But forgiveness—from God, toward yourself, and toward others—is essential to the process of healing. It's part of the great gift God longs to give you. It's the key to the spiritual and emotional freedom that is available, just around the corner.

There are ways to sort out the tangled strands that bind your heart. It is possible to release the resentment, to reconcile relationships, to find forgiveness. Read on. We'll help you do it.

Forgiveness from God

The foundational issue to address is forgiveness from God. If you haven't found forgiveness in Him, you will never find lasting peace. It simply isn't available from any other source.

For some of you, that statement drains you of hope. How, you wonder, could God possibly forgive me? How could I even face Him with this? How could I even dare to ask?

If those are your thoughts, they are not coming from God in His Word. What the Bible does offer is a portrait—in fact, a gallery of portraits, page after page of them—of your Father's open arms, of His compassionate face, all with captions affirming in strong language that *there is no sin greater than His capacity to forgive.* Want to see a few of them? Take a look:

> You are forgiving and good, O Lord, abounding in love to all who call to you (Ps. 86:5).

> Praise the Lord, O my soul, and forget not all his benefits— who forgives *all* your sins and heals *all* your diseases, who redeems your life from the pit and crowns you with love and compassion (Ps. 103:2-4, emphasis added).

> Who is a God like you, who pardons sin and forgives the transgression . . . ? You do not stay angry forever but delight to show mercy. You will again have compassion on us; you will tread our sins underfoot and hurl *all* our iniquities into the depths of the sea (Micah 7:18-19, emphasis added).

> Repent, then, and turn to God, so that your sins may be wiped out, that times of refreshing may come from the Lord, and that he may send the Christ, who has been appointed for you—even Jesus (Acts 3:19-20).

> "Come now, let us reason together," says the Lord. "Though your sins are like scarlet, they shall be as white as snow; though they are red as crimson, they shall be like wool" (Isa 1:18).

> If we confess our sins, he is faithful and just and will forgive us our sins and purify us from all unrighteousness (1 John 1:9).

God's forgiveness hinges only on one thing: our acknowledgment of our own sin. What often keeps us from it? Fear. Look at your other relationships. Maybe you have found it too hard to tell certain people in your life about your abortion. Perhaps it has been your mother's disappointment that you find difficult to face. Maybe it's the look of betrayal on your husband's face that you can't bear to see. Maybe you're afraid of the reaction of your friends if they were ever to find out.

With God, however, there needn't be any fear for two important reasons. First, He already knows about your abortion. You can't shock or surprise Him. He not only knows what you did, but He was there when it happened.

Yes, you read that right.

When you conceived that child, He was there.

When you discovered you were pregnant, He was there.

When you tossed and turned, cried and prayed, panicked and planned, He was there. Did you hear His voice? Did your fear drown it out? Did you close your ears? He knows that too. He knows the worst and the most pitiable about those awful days. He knew even then what you would decide and yet He stayed. His love for you continued.

When you entered the abortion clinic, as you lay on that table, your boyfriend may have been in the car, your mother may have been in the waiting room, but *He was there*, all the time. With you. With your baby. This is confirmed by Psalm 139:8: "If I go up to the heavens, you are there; if I make my bed in the depths, you are there."

There is nothing you have done that He doesn't know, didn't see. He waits only for you to acknowledge it. But you can do so without fear, because of the second difference: *You know His response.*

You can't be sure how your friends or your husband or your mother will react. But you can be sure how God will react. He will forgive. He will rejoice. He'll throw a party, and invite all the angels! If you don't believe it, read the story of the prodigal son in Luke 15:11-24: "For this son of mine was dead and is alive again; he was lost and is found. So they began to celebrate."

Don't forget, He is used to sinners, as Romans 3:23 says: "For all have sinned and fall short of the glory of God." He hasn't turned one away yet.

Forgiving Ourselves

The pain of a past abortion can be the worst form of self-torture existing in the world. If you have other children, the very pleasure they bring may deepen your sense of loss. Little league games, piano recitals, Christmas choirs all remind you of what might have been.

If you have no living children, the loss may be even more intense. You may find yourself avoiding parks, schools, church nurseries in hopes of avoiding the ache of longing they arouse.

Though millions of women share your anguish, only you know the true cost of your abortion. The price has been subtracted from your heart in hundreds of ways, the loss of the child being the most obvious. You may feel tortured with regret over your own loss of innocence, over the things you've done in order to cope, over the secrets you've had to keep, and over the physical consequences of the procedure. You likely had your abortion so that your life would not have to change. In reality, the abortion, itself, forced changes. Changes you never would have chosen.

Even if your life has gone more smoothly than it might have had you not chosen to abort, there is still the fact of the abortion itself. Perhaps you feel secretly guilty for having gone on to attain the things you wanted, when they have been paid for with your child's life.

No matter what pressures you faced, regardless of what misinformation you'd been given, deep down, you know that the decision was yours. For many women, that truth haunts them like a ghost.

But if God, whose standards are holier than yours, whose hopes for you were even higher than your own—if He has forgiven you, can you not forgive yourself?

Jesus wants so much for you to be free from your sins that He died to make it possible. In John 10:10 He tells us, "I have come that they may have life, and have it to the full." You don't need to atone for your abortion by feeling guilty for the rest of your life. The whole point of Christianity is that we could never atone for our sins, whether they are great or small. That's why Jesus came. That's what the Cross is all about.

Please, won't you reach out to God and pray. Receive His forgiveness, and begin to forgive yourself.

Forgiving Others

You didn't get pregnant by yourself, and you didn't choose abortion by yourself.

Some of the people involved in your decision know they were involved—those who counseled you, and naturally, the abortionist himself. Others may not even know an abortion took place, but they, too, played a role. Maybe you never told your parents, your boyfriend, or your friends that you were pregnant . . . but you had the abortion so that you never would have to tell them. In your heart, you still hold them partially responsible. After all if they'd been more supportive in other matters, you might have felt able to go to them with this one.

Maybe you were young and it was your parents' wishes, even demands, that you get an abortion. Maybe they took you to the clinics without considering what your wishes might be. You had to obey them.

Yes, the ultimate responsibility is yours. But that doesn't mean it is yours alone. Those who influenced you, wittingly or unwittingly, to make that decision, bear the guilt as well. And though you may be forgiven for your part, *you will never be entirely free until you have forgiven them for their part too.*

It's one thing when the person asks to be forgiven. There's something about an apology that makes forgiveness flow more freely. But what about when they really don't have any remorse for their actions against you? What if they do not even comprehend the wrong that they have done? That's when forgiveness sticks in your throat.

Why is that? Perhaps it's because forgiveness without repentance feels like acceptance of the wrong done. It feels as if you are saying, "That's okay," when it isn't okay. When it was a big deal.

God never asks us to approve what was done, to condone the wrong. He just wants us to stop holding them accountable for it—and let Him hold them accountable instead. As we're reminded in Romans 14:10, "we will all stand before God's judgment seat."

The commands in Scripture to forgive others are numerous:

- "If you hold anything against anyone, forgive him" (Mark 11:25).
- ". . . be reconciled to your brother" (Matt. 5:23).
- "I tell you . . . seventy-seven times" (Matt. 18:22).

The list goes on and on.

It often feels like a tall order. But God never asks us to do anything that is not, ultimately, good for us. Do you know how the dictionary defines the word forgive? "To renounce anger or resentment against an offender."[1]

Wouldn't that be nice? Imagine it. To cease to feel resentment . . . to cease to feel resentment . . . When was the last time you experienced that, the absence of resentment? Do you even remember what it was like?

Your heavenly Father would like you to be experiencing that now. He's not asking you to say it didn't matter. It did matter. If you were lied to, misinformed, it mattered. If you were pressured or threatened, it mattered. If you felt alone, afraid, in danger of rejection, it mattered. If you were made to feel responsible for someone else's emotional well being, it mattered. It mattered to God then, and it matters to Him now. His forgiveness is available to those people, but that is between them and Him. What He asks is that you put the burden of resentment in His hands. Forgive them. Let them off the hook in your heart, and allow God to put them on His hook, to deal with in His own way.

As you do so, ask Him to show you a new way to view those people, new insights into who they are and why. And too, ask Him to show you what responsibility you might have in the tensions that did, or perhaps still do, exist in those relationships. He'd like few things more than to clear the slate between you and those people—to replace resentment with understanding and reconciliation.

Make a list of everyone who had a part, big or small, known or unknown, in your abortion decision. Explore thoroughly your reasons for resenting them. Then pray through your list, asking God to help you see them in a new light, to forgive them, and to turn them over to Him for repayment of their debt.

> *I knew I needed to forgive my mother, yet anger toward her consumed me. I asked God to reveal to me ways that I might have hurt her as well, and He reminded me that I had killed her grandchild, robbed her of him without even considering her feelings. And on top of that, I had blamed her for it. As I realized this, my heart toward her began to change and soften. The understanding that God forgave me made forgiving her so much easier because I realized she wasn't responsible for my abortion decision.*
>
> —Sydna

Blessed is he
whose transgressions are forgiven,
whose sins are covered.
Blessed is the man
whose sin the Lord does not count against him
and in whose spirit is no deceit.
When I kept silent,
my bones wasted away
through my groaning all day long.
For day and night
your hand was heavy upon me;
my strength was sapped
as in the heat of summer.
Then I acknowledged my sin to you
and did not cover up my iniquity.
I said, "I will confess
my transgressions to the Lord"—
and you forgave
the guilt of my sin.
Therefore let everyone who is godly pray to you
while you may be found;
surely when the mighty waters rise,
they will not reach him.
You are my hiding place;

you will protect me from trouble
and surround me with songs of deliverance.

(Ps. 32:1-7)

Get rid of all bitterness, rage and anger, brawling and slander,
along with every form of malice.
Be kind and compassionate to one another, forgiving each other,
just as in Christ God forgave you.

(Eph. 4:31-32)

a healing place

C.S. Lewis once said:

> To forgive for the moment is not difficult. But to go on forgiving, to forgive the same offense every time it recurs to the memory—there's the real tussle.[2]

Use the space provided to make a list of those you need to forgive. As you pray through the list, be as specific as possible about the hurt and forgiveness you are offering each individual. And be prepared, as Lewis said, for the "real tussle."

CHAPTER 7

joy comes in the mourning: letting go at last

Forget the former things; do not dwell on the past.
See, I am doing a new thing! Now it springs up;
do you not perceive it?
I am making a way in the desert and streams
in the wasteland.

(Isa. 43:18-19)

After my abortion, I eventually met and married a wonderful man with whom I had three children. I even began working with the Crisis Pregnancy Center ministry at Focus on the Family in a desire to help other women who were going through what I had experienced. Life began to feel good, yet the flashbacks continued, and the ache in my heart would not go away. A series of events led me into a P.A.C.E. (Post Abortion Counseling and Education) Bible study at the Colorado Springs Pregnancy Center. Through the Bible study I dealt with and found relief from the myriad emotions associated with my past. I felt as though I was shedding layer after layer of dead skin. It was painful, but a new person was coming to life within me—a new person who was free! But there was one thing left to do. I had found the courage to face my emotions and

release them; now it was time to face my long-lost baby . . .
and release him as well.

—Sydna

While it sometimes seems impossible to believe, there is a way to joy after an abortion. In mourning your loss, confessing your sin, forgiving yourself and others involved in your abortion decision, God's peace can come through and joy can once again fill your soul.

But there is one thing left to take care of. One more issue to confront. You've made things right with God; you've begun to forgive yourself; you're on the road to forgiving others . . . and now you need to make things right with your lost child. You need to answer the questions that plague your soul, and you need to say good-bye—at least, for now.

Confronting the Questions

It's one thing to deal with the tangible issues surrounding our abortions—feeling anger toward flesh-and-blood people; asking forgiveness from God whose Word assures us of His answer. But it's another thing altogether to come to the heart of what hurts . . . wondering what has happened to this child whom we were supposed to protect, and how that baby regards us now. The questions are almost too fearful to face, but you'll never be fully at rest until you know the answers.

Where Is My Baby Now?

What a terrible guilt many struggle with because they are uncertain what happened to their babies! If a child dies before accepting Jesus, where does he go? Can she possibly find a home in heaven? How can we know for sure?

Scripture does address this issue. Jesus certainly welcomed children. Remember when the disciples tried to keep the little ones from bothering Him? His response, in Matthew 19:14, was a rebuke: "Let the little children come to me, and do not hinder them, for the kingdom of heaven belongs to such as these."

This is a comforting passage to parents. But for the one who has aborted a child, an even more reassuring passage is found once again in 2 Samuel, the story of David and Bathsheba. If ever there was a crisis pregnancy, theirs was. Soon after their child was born he became gravely ill. David, finally aware of the tragedies he had set in motion, was wild with grief. He fasted and mourned for his son until, finally, the child died. Why did he stop then? Surely now his grief must be greater than ever. 2 Samuel 12:22-24 tells us why. And his reason is one we, too, can cling to.

> While the child was still alive, I fasted and wept. I thought, 'Who knows? The Lord may be gracious to me and let the child live.' But now that he is dead, why should I fast? Can I bring him back again? *I will go to him, but he will not return to me*" (emphasis added).

The hope in this verse is implied, but it is real nonetheless. David, certainly, expected to spend eternity in heaven, despite his sin. His many psalms tell of his absolute trust in God's mercy and forgiveness. In stating that he (David) expects to go to him (his baby), David makes it clear that he believes his son is with the Lord in heaven. There was no debate—just calm assurance that he would see his boy again.

Nowhere in Scripture is there a single verse indicating that babies, even those conceived out of wedlock, are unwelcome in the home of their Heavenly Father. Rest assured that your little one is safe in the arms of Jesus.

How Does My Baby Feel about Me?

Do you believe that your child might hate you for taking his or her life? This is another common facet of the post-abortion experience. There is often a deep dread of death, because it means we will come face to face with the children we aborted.

Frank Peretti has written a novel called *Tilly*. It is the fictional account of a dream in which a mother meets her aborted child. The child, named Tilly, attempts to bring her mother to an understanding of what life in heaven is all about. There is not sorrow, judgment, or hatred, only joy filling each day. The children there harbor no bitterness. They don't miss life on earth; they only desire that their earthly parents not be filled with sorrow.[1]

Peretti's book does not pretend to be a Bible study, but it is consistent with what we find in Scripture about heaven. And what a wonderful picture it presents of our children's life there. Only God is the judge in heaven—not our children. They have been released from Satan's grip and are not plagued by the darkness which seeks to disrupt the Holy Spirit's peaceful presence in our hearts.

Another human perspective on the aborted child's viewpoint comes from Christian recording artist Kathy Troccoli. Her Dove award-winning song "A Baby's Prayer" (1998—"Most Inspirational Song") shares the love a soon-to-be-aborted child has for her mother:

I can hear her talking with a friend
I think it's all about me
Oh how she can't have a baby now
My mommy doesn't see

That I feel her breathe
I know her voice
Her blood, it flows through my heart
God, you know my greatest wish is that
We'd never be apart

But if I should die before I wake
I pray her soul you'll keep
Forgive her Lord—she doesn't know
That you gave life to me

Do I really have to say good-bye
Don't want this time to be through
Oh please tell her that I love her Lord
And that you love her too

Cause if I should die before I wake
I pray her soul you'll keep
Forgive her Lord, she doesn't know
That you gave life to me.

On the day that she might think of me
Please comfort her with the truth
That the angels hold me safe and sound
Cause I'm in heaven with you
I'm in heaven with you.[2]

It's hard to know what heaven will be like exactly, but with God's help, you can know that your lost child will be very happy to meet you at last. Instead of dreading that day when you look in his eyes, you can look forward with joy to the moment you first hold her in your arms.

For many post-abortive women, it's very healing to sit down and write a letter to their child. By pouring out your sorrow directly to your child, apologizing, and acknowledging him or her as a human being, a vital step in mourning is realized. Had your child lived he or she would have imparted great value upon the world and fulfilled a purpose God had designed just for that child. Realizing this at first deepens your grief, but in doing so you can begin to mourn in the normal human fashion.

Mourning Your Loss

Mourning may not sound like a very pleasant proposition. It sounds like something that would deepen your grief, not lessen it! But the surprising thing is, mourning sets you free. Maybe that's why funerals and wakes and the like are such an intricate part of virtually every human culture—they help us accept and process the loss of something precious in our lives.

When you aborted your baby, it's unlikely that you allowed yourself to consciously grieve. After all, who grieves the loss of a lump of tissue?

Give yourself the opportunity to mourn in a deliberate way. There is no prescribed formula for making this happen however, so we will provide some suggestions later in this chapter. Whatever you choose, you first will need to identify, at least to yourself, the person you are memorializing.

Giving Your Child a Name

When you have worked for years to keep the memory of the abortion away from your heart, thinking about the baby as a real human being is amazing. The simple task of giving your child a name is a great way to begin.

> *The post-abortion Bible study suggested that we name our aborted children, but, though I was sure my baby was a boy, I couldn't name him no matter how hard I tried. On the way to class I prayed, "Help me with this, Lord." Deep in my heart I heard His answer.*
>
> *"Your son has been in heaven for eleven years. Don't you think I've named him by now? He's called Jesse."*
>
> *That was it! His names was Jesse! It was simple and sweet. God had already named my son. He cared for every aborted child in*

heaven—enough to give each one a name when their parents couldn't even realize that they were children. And my son's name was special. It was King David's father's name—and Jesus was a descendent from Jesse. God had cared enough to give my son a special name. I would later discover that the name, Jesse, means "God exists" in Hebrew.

—Sydna

Ways to Memorialize Your Child

Choosing a memorial as a way of remembering your child is an integral part of healing, although the tears may flow for days or weeks. Initially you may recoil from the thought of it. However before you reject the idea, read this chapter. There are as many ways to memorialize a child as there are children. You may want to hold a small, private funeral service; you might want to plant a tree; you may want to write a poem, make a donation to a charity, write his or her story in a journal . . . the choice is purely personal.

Sydna's Memorial

When our post-abortion Bible study leaders suggested that, as a group, we hold a memorial service for our aborted babies, most of us nearly fell off our chairs. I immediately vowed that I would not attend. Recognizing our lack of confidence, they asked us to trust them—that this would be a good experience. They suggested that we bring a candle for each aborted baby and a bouquet of flowers.

The day of the service, I felt sick. I stayed home from work to prepare. Michael's birth had been nine months earlier, and I had saved a wicker basket shaped like a bassinet from one of the flower arrangements I had received. From garden flowers, I made an arrangement with a candle-holder in the middle.

My husband wasn't sure that this was such a good idea but

offered to go with me. Sensing his apprehension, I figured it would be better to go alone than to worry about his comfort during the service. Instead, I took my baby, Michael, with me. I felt that I needed a family member present. It's funny how much moral support young children can be!

I carried Michael into the church and found it beautifully lighted. I placed Jesse's bassinet basket on the altar and marveled at how beautiful the arrangements looked. It was a peaceful place and I was immediately at rest in my heart. Unfortunately, Michael began to fuss, so my group leader, Melissa, took him and walked him in the back of the sanctuary for most of the service. I was grateful for her assistance and his presence.

Music played quietly as the pastor began the service. Most captivating to me was a passage he read from John 11:43-44 about Lazarus:

> Jesus called in a loud voice, "Lazarus, come out!" The dead man came out, his hands and feet wrapped with strips of linen, and a cloth around his face. Jesus said to them, "Take off the grave clothes and let him go."

The pastor then said, "I want to compare you to the risen Lazarus. You are very much alive inside but still tightly bound by the grave clothes—your children. We are simply here as friends to help you remove these grave clothes."

As I sat there, I realized immediately that I had felt very bound by Jesse's death. The pastor's analysis made perfect sense. I went to pray with him, and he simply asked the Lord to remove these grave clothes. Within that minute, I felt like I had lost thirty pounds! The bondage of this sin was removed and I was free at last.

When I sat down, Melissa brought Michael to me and I hugged him closely. I had never expected joy from this event but that was what I was feeling. The words to the old hymn became true in those following moments:

Heaven came down and glory filled my soul
When at the cross my Savior made me whole.
My sins were washed away,
And my night was turned to day.
Heaven came down and glory filled my soul.[3]

As I sat there, waiting for the other women to pray, I pondered what my child was feeling in heaven at that moment. For a brief second, as I closed my eyes, I saw what looked like the silhouette of a boy with his hands raised in the air as if he were cheering. I asked God what this was and felt an immediate response: "All of heaven is rejoicing; you've come home!" I couldn't help but wonder if the silhouette was my own Jesse cheering me on, saying, "Go Mom!"

Joan's Memorial

When you have experienced multiple abortions, healing may come harder. There are more memories, some deeply buried, and it simply takes longer to work them all through. You may want to follow the steps in this book separately for each abortion, since the situations and pain revolving around each experience can differ greatly. Likewise, you may want to memorialize each child separately, and perhaps differently as well. It's up to you.

The healing of my heart took place in what I believe to be the most dramatic, emotional, and spiritual experience of my life. That is when I became intimately acquainted with my Savior, realizing His love for me and how precious His redemption now seemed to be.

Previously I had completed a Post-Abortion Counseling and Education class and even helped facilitate classes. I had the head knowledge for healing the wounds of abortion. I even planted three aspen trees in my yard, one for each child, and watched their branches mature quickly, reaching toward heaven. But I couldn't seem to get past the pain in my heart. There was no rest for me. I agonized over the tragedy of three babies lost to abortion.

In the book, *Will I Cry Tomorrow?*, Dr. Susan Stanford-Rue had written of her own abortion experience and the inner healing that had finally brought her peace. When I read of her experience, I wanted that peace. I needed that peace. I didn't think it could be possible for me, but I asked Sue, the crisis pregnancy center director, if she and Melissa, our P.A.C.E. administrator, would help me.

What I experienced was unusual and probably will not happen to you. The Lord knows each of us, healing us in different ways.

I will remember that day forever—March 28, 1989. It had been the anniversary week of one of my abortions. While Melissa prayed, Sue led me back to the "scene of the crime" so to speak. The first abortion was where it all started. It was then that I remembered everything and reexperienced the abortion.

At long last the dam broke. Tears poured uncontrollably down my face. For the first time in seven years I was crying. Really crying! I could not stop myself. All the pain and heartache of all those years was coming to the surface and overflowing. I was finally able to grieve for my children. I needed to mourn the loss of my children.

Sue asked me what I was experiencing. As I described the details, I ached for the innocence that was lost in that abortion clinic in 1976. Closing my eyes, I remembered the procedure, I thought of the nurse holding my hand, and I looked up into her face. But it was not her face that I saw—it was Jesus, and He was smiling! He was standing there next to me. His eyes were filled with love and compassion. The warmth that penetrated from His being filled my soul.

"Don't you know that I have been with you all along?" He said gently. He was holding a little blue bundle. I could see little arms waving back and forth.

"Here is your son." Handing me the bundle, He stepped back and swung His arm outward with a sweeping motion. As I looked, I saw all of heaven open up. The colors were brilliant. Crystal blue skies, green rolling hills with flowers, and CHILDREN! Hundreds of children, laughing, bright and happy. I knew instinctively that these were aborted children. But they were whole! Not mutilated and torn the way I had pictured my own children. They were safe and whole with Jesus.

Amazingly, standing in front of them was my first husband, Bob, who had died years earlier. Jesus took the blue bundle from my arms and handed him to his father. Then He turned back to me. This time He was holding two pink bundles—my little girls. Suddenly the vision was gone and so were my tears of sorrow. They were now tears of joy. The peace that filled my heart was a peace I had never known. I knew God had worked the ultimate miracle in my life. Just as Psalm 40 said, He had redeemed my life from the pit. He put a new song in my heart.

He also put these words in my mind as I penned:

I see my son
Wrapped in blue;
Safe in Jesus' arms
Whole and new.
What is this gift so undeserved,
This glimpse into heaven
When the horror of my sin has me so unnerved?
I see my son,
His little arms waving back and forth
As though telling me in heaven he is of great worth.
"Don't cry for me," they seem to say.
"I love you, Mom. It's okay."
I see my son now
With peace and love
Ever grateful to Jesus
For the precious assurance of heaven above.

Another way to memorialize your child

Recently, while I (Joan) was co-leading a post-abortion Bible study, the other leader introduced the concept of building a scrapbook to memorialize our children. I have to say, the idea sounded almost morbid to me. Admitting to the group I had never indulged in this exercise, we took on the endeavor together over the next several weeks.

Finding pictures, words, and phrases from magazines, we cut out the "story of our lives," including events and feelings that led to the abortion experience, as well as the aftermath. I was amazed at how, from *Newsweek* to *LIFE* to *American Baby*, my own life played out through the cut-out words and pictures. This scrapbook has become a precious memento of a season of my life, chronicling the guilt, shame, and pain that grew into a life filled with peace and joy as I found healing through the unbreakable bond of love from my Heavenly Father.

Your Own Happy Ending

We know that very few women will have a dramatic event such as a vision. God will specialize His work in your heart in a way He knows will bring you the most peace.

Certainly everyone is not able or required to have an actual funeral service for her children, or make scrapbooks or plant a tree. Feel free to create something out of your own special talents. A tangible memorial can be very comforting—just like visiting the graveside of a beloved friend.

Whatever way you are led to remember your child, please step forward in faith and participate in some sort of memorial. As the years go by, it will remind you that you have honored your child, provided him or her with the human dignity of being named, and shed tears on the child's behalf. God's strong embrace through this process will strengthen and enrich your life and future relationships And, most of all, it will bring you peace and hope for your future.

A year later I felt led to put Jesse's name on a plaque at the National Memorial for the Unborn, in Chattanooga, Tennessee. I had become friends with Linda Keener and Pat Lindsay, the directors of this memorial. It was housed at a former abortion clinic, the very spot where thirty-five thousand children had lost their lives.

I marveled at the site of this special place and was reminded of the Scripture in Genesis 50:20: "You intended to harm me, but God intended it for good to accomplish what is now being done, the saving of many lives."

But I had only a first name for my son. I struggled with the knowledge that Jesse's father probably still did not mourn his loss and I felt using his last name wouldn't be appropriate.

Out of the blue I received a call from my boyfriend's father, a Methodist pastor who had heard about my abortion from my mother years earlier. I had sent this lovely man a broadcast tape of my story two years earlier but had never heard from him. He relayed that he and his wife rarely shared about this loss and that she couldn't speak to me over the phone. They were still grieving. He said his son had just married a woman with two older children and so had probably aborted his only child. Then he finished the conversation by saying that they had forgiven me and were very proud of my efforts against abortion.

As I hung up the phone, it was clear that Jesse's name was complete. He would bear the name of his grandfather who loved him dearly. I was struck by the depth of this grandfather's pain and my role in causing this grief. My mother paid the suggested donation for the plaque and had only one request—that the simple word "REDEEMED" be on the third line.

—Sydna

I have set the Lord always before me.
Because he is at my right hand,
I will not be shaken.
Therefore my heart is glad and my tongue rejoices;
my body also will rest secure,
because you will not abandon me to the grave,
nor will you let your Holy One see decay.
You have made known to me the path of life;
you will fill me with joy in your presence,
with eternal pleasures at your right hand.

(Ps. 16:8-11)

a healing place

Denial, anger, depression, acceptance, these are all stages in the grieving process. And no two people grieve in the same way or in the same order. Just remember that the goal of mourning is not to "get over" it but to get through it—to do the work of grieving. Choosing a way to memorialize your child can be a significant step in that process. When you're ready, use the space provided to record the memorial you created and the feelings that it brought to the surface.

CHAPTER 8

where do I go from here?

He has sent me to bind up the brokenhearted,
to proclaim freedom for the captives and release from
darkness for the prisoners, . . . to comfort all who mourn,
and provide for those who grieve in Zion—to bestow
on them a crown of beauty instead of ashes, the oil of
gladness instead of mourning, and a garment
of praise instead of a spirit of despair.

(Isa. 61:1-3)

The call came through the counseling lines at Focus on the Family, and the phone was handed to me. It was a woman who was considering abortion. What on earth was I to say to her? I felt totally out of my element. Terror filled my heart as I realized my words might be the only thing standing between this little child and death. I said a quick prayer and listened as she told me her story.

She was pregnant from a one-night encounter, and she was already the single mother of three girls. One of her daughters was thirteen, and the mother was afraid that if her daughter found out about the pregnancy, all hope of her choosing an abstinent lifestyle would be gone.

I shared with this woman about the pain that abortion brings and prayed with her, but as we hung up, she still leaned toward ending the pregnancy. For two weeks, Joan and I prayed for this young mother and called her frequently. The day before her abortion appointment, she was still planning to go through with it. We prayed fervently for her that evening, and the next day, when Joan called, she was at home! She had changed her mind at the last minute.

Seven months later, a message on my desk contained these words about this woman's delivery:

It's a boy!
7 lbs. 19 oz.
19 inches long
His name is . . . Jesse!

This mother had no idea what I had named my lost son, but her little Jesse was proof positive that my Jesse had not died in vain.

—Sydna

If reading through these chapters has touched your heart, then our prayers have been answered. In the warmth and security of your own home, God has come down into your heart and begun the work of His healing. But your journey doesn't end there.

Continuing Your Own Healing

You have done a lot of work in your heart since you began reading this book. You have likely shed many tears, fought through much pain, dredged up many memories you'd really rather have forgotten. An experience like abortion is not an easy one to put behind you.

You've made a wonderful start on the road to healing, and a brave one. Probably you are feeling a greater degree of peace than you have sensed in a long time. But there is no comfort like that which you can receive from God's people—the brothers and sisters in Christ who have also survived an abortion experience. We encourage you to join a post-abortion Bible study in your area and experience the bond that shared grief can bring. The women you will find there will understand a part of you that has lived in isolation since the day of your abortion.

Currently there are more than 3,200 Crisis Pregnancy Centers in the United States. They provide free pregnancy tests, maternity and baby clothes, furniture, housing, parenting classes, and friendship. Another tier of their service is in the area of reconciliation—post-abortion ministry. Most are located under the "Abortions Alternatives" section of the yellow pages. Call and ask them about the services they offer to struggling post-abortive individuals. In most cases, your call will be completely confidential and you will be treated with love, compassion, and care.

Go and visit the center and pray about joining whatever program it offers on post-abortion trauma. Ask specifically to be introduced to other post-abortive individuals and strike up friendships wherever possible. Also, begin to put out some feelers within your own circle of friends. The Alan Guttmacher Institute (Planned Parenthood's former research group) estimates that 43 percent of American women have had at least one abortion by the age of forty-five.[1] Chances are good that you know some of them! The blessings that will come from these relationships will be treasures to you in the years to come. And as you continue to work through your abortion issues, remember Philippians 1:6: "He who began a good work in you will carry it on to completion . . ."

Telling the Secret

If you are like most post-abortive women, there are significant people in your life who do not know that you have had an abortion.

There may be good reasons for your silence. But then again, the reason may be pure and simple fear. Do you find that this secret is eroding some of your relationships? Does it stand between you and true intimacy with someone in your life? Perhaps it is time to take this particular scrapbook off the shelf and open it up. The time may or may not be right, but it is certainly something to prayerfully consider, especially with regard to your immediate family.

How Sydna Told Her Story

In the years following my abortion, I told several people about it, including Tom, who later became my husband. However, I did not tell some of the most significant people in my life—my parents and my boyfriend's parents among them.

Of course, many members of my Focus on the Family "family" knew all about it. After all, I did work in their Crisis Pregnancy Center division. As a requirement for my job, I had to take the P.A.C.E. class that was so instrumental in my healing, and I had shared my story in a devotional time at work. But the day came when a call came from our broadcasting department asking for a testimonial from someone who had experienced an abortion. Facetiously, I offered, "You can always use mine." One thing led to another, and I soon found myself in front of a tape recorder sharing the same testimony I had given at devotions the week before. The tape, which contained my name, would air on the Focus on the Family radio program in four months. I could just imagine my family tuning in and finding out, along with five- to ten-million other listeners, what I had done. I knew I would have to tell them in advance.

I was thankful that my children were too little to be told. But I sent my mother, father, and friends a copy of the tape, along with a letter of explanation. I even sent one to my boyfriend and his family. And then I waited for their response.

I wasn't surprised at the response from most people—silence. But I did receive some unexpectedly wonderful responses, including one from my mother's best friend and, eventually, one from my former boyfriend's father. My mother's response was one of hurt, particularly since, on the tape, I had unwittingly made it sound as if she had known I was pregnant. It was not easy telling people the truth, and some of those relationships will never be the same. But for every friend that was lost during that time, ten more were added. I was surrounded by prayer and love from these gracious individuals, and I look forward to the day when the hurt I both caused and experienced around the time of my abortion will be completely erased.

How Joan Told Her Story to Her Son

My two older boys, having lived through that horrible time with me, knew about my abortions. But now their two little brothers (from my second marriage to Bill) were growing up, and I suspected the time was coming to tell them as well. But when? And how?

In my work at Focus on the Family, these questions came up continually from post-abortive women. We always suggested prayer; if God provided the opportunity to talk about it, then they were to follow His leading. I decided to take my own advice, and I began to pray for God to show me when the time would be right to tell Steven and Daniel.

The opportunity to tell Steven came sooner than anticipated and in a way I had least expected. It was a bright, sunshiny spring day. Steven, who was eleven at the time, had several friends over and they were all playing in the backyard. I went about my business as I periodically checked on them outside. Suddenly, I noticed there was silence. I looked out the window and saw no one.

When I went out, I could hear voices coming from their little clubhouse. I thought, I'll just sneak up and listen. *I'll probably catch them playing with matches or something.* As I tiptoed up to the clubhouse I distinctly heard one boy say, "Look at that girl's . . ." I didn't wait for the rest of the sentence, but flung open the door and very calmly said, "Hand it over." The boys handed me two magazines that were more than pornographic; they were sadistic. I felt a wave of sickness pass through me. I ordered all the boys to go home and Steven to come inside.

His father and I explained to him that these magazines were degrading to women and that very sick people published these things. We also explained how they can affect the minds of young boys, prompting them to do very mean things to women when they grow up to be men.

Steven was consumed with guilt. He said he felt sick and was sure that everyone could see right through him, knowing the truth about what he had done. Then he said, "I bet you've never done anything as bad as this, Mom."

"Oh, dear Lord," I thought, "is this the time, the opportunity that I prayed for to share about the abortions? Okay, here goes."

I told Steven that I, too, had done something bad in my life. Something I thought was even worse.

"You know how I don't like abortion and help women with abortion decisions? Well, that's because I had an abortion. In fact, I had three. I didn't know the truth about abortion. I didn't know what it would do to me or that they were really babies. I believed the lies that they were just blobs of tissue."

"So I have a brother in heaven?" Steven responded.

"Yes, I believe God has shown me that you have a brother and two sisters in heaven."

"But you've always told me that one sin isn't any worse than another, that they are all the same in God's eyes. So what you did isn't any worse than what I did."

Out of the mouths of babes! Not only had God used Steven's

transgression to open the door for truth between us, but He had used his words to remind me of a very important truth—all sin *is* the same in God's eyes; we are all on common ground at the foot of the cross.

This was a very emotional time of bonding for the two of us. We prayed and hugged and forgave each other our shortcomings and asked God to forgive us and reconcile us to Him.

Telling Your Story

If you have been wondering if you should tell your children or other loved ones, ask the Lord to open the door of opportunity. You may feel that this truth would encourage a future abortion in your children's lives. We have found the opposite to be true. How horrible it is when a post-abortive mother becomes a post-abortive grandmother, that is, when her daughter continues the cycle. Honesty is the only way to break the possibility in their lives. In most cases, the pain you express to them about your own abortion will lead them to avoid that choice. You may become the only human being they can turn to should they find themselves in a crisis pregnancy.

Participating in Others' Healing

Imagine yourself, back at the time of your unplanned pregnancy, walking into a Christian center that provided you with an accurate picture of the consequences of abortion. Should you have been fearful of your parents' reaction, the compassionate women there would have gone with you to help you break the news. At all points in your pregnancy, they would have stood by you and offered help in whatever way necessary. These gracious, God-fearing individuals would also have been there as you delivered your precious baby into the world. They would have helped you get started raising your little one, or would have supported you in going through with an adoption.

Wouldn't that have been better than the alternative you ended up with? You can be that compassionate, gracious, God-fearing person for another woman.

Many of you have cried multitudes of tears since first opening the cover of this book. Though there may be more healing yet to come in your life, already you have something to offer other women, who, like yourself, have experienced the pain and regret of abortion. And you certainly have much to offer women who are at the crossroads, facing an unplanned pregnancy and uncertain what to do.

Can you imagine the incredible feeling of holding a baby that God used you to save? To know that this baby would have surely died and God intervened with your testimony to save her life is a joy few realize in a lifetime. Whatever your gifts, whether you are good at public speaking, raising money, teaching classes, organizing workers, folding baby blankets, or drying tears, God can use you. And Crisis Pregnancy Centers across the country have a place for you.

CPCs have an extensive training program for their volunteer counseling staff. Most also offer prayer coverage and friendship to every volunteer regardless of their role. The Lord's presence is very powerful in these centers and His ministry through you can be one of the most rewarding in your life.

I was at the funeral of an old friend, sitting in the back pew by myself. My keyring was a medal that had an impression of the "Precious Feet." They are the actual size of a baby's feet at ten weeks gestation. I was about to put my key ring in my purse when I was suddenly compelled to lay it beside me on the pew.

Within five minutes a young woman whom I had never seen before, sat down next to me. As the service ended, she turned to me and said, "I noticed your key ring. I had an abortion eight years ago. My husband divorced me a year later and I've never remarried. It was probably the only child that I will ever conceive." She was in obvious pain, and my heart opened up to her. I shared with her briefly that I, too, had an abortion and how it had consumed me for years, but God, in His grace, had led me to a place where I found healing. Experiences like this one have occurred time and again since then. I am so grateful that God has taken my sin and turned it into a tool for His own compassionate use.

—Joan

You may be surprised how God provides opportunities to participate in the healing of other women. However He does it, God can use YOU for His ultimate purpose of healing.

Be at rest once more, O my soul,
for the Lord has been good to you. . . .
How can I repay the Lord
for all his goodness to me?
I will lift up the cup of salvation
and call on the name of the Lord.
I will fulfill my vows to the Lord
in the presence of all his people.
Precious in the sight of the Lord
is the death of his saints.
O Lord truly I am your servant; . . .
you have freed me from my chains.
I will sacrifice a thank offering to you
and call on the name of the Lord.

(Ps. 116:7, 12-17)

a healing place

Proverbs 11:25 states, "He who refreshes others will himself be refreshed." God uses our efforts to help others to bring even further healing to ourselves. Perhaps you're not ready to reach out—that's okay. But sooner or later reaching out to others with the same comfort you've received will become an important part of your own healing and ministry.

Pray that the Apostle Paul's words in 2 Corinthians 1:3-4 will be true in your life.

> Praise be to the God and Father of our Lord Jesus Christ, the Father of compassion and the God of all comfort, who comforts us in all our troubles, so that we can comfort those in any trouble with the comfort we ourselves have received from God.

Do you know Jesus?

To find complete peace from your abortion experience, you need to have a personal relationship with Jesus Christ. His love is available to everyone—even someone who has chosen abortion. If you have never asked Jesus into your heart, you can do so right now. The path of salvation is relayed in John 3:16 and Romans 10:9:

> *"For God so loved the world that he gave his one and only Son, that whoever believes in him shall not perish but have eternal life."*

> *"That if you confess with your mouth, 'Jesus is Lord,' and believe in your heart that God raised him from the dead, you will be saved."*

Do you want an intimate relationship with Jesus? These scriptures are your blueprint for salvation. Open your heart and believe in Him.

epilogue

by Stephen Arterburn
President and Founder, New Life Clinics

You may find it strange that this book would end with words from a man. I hope you will not allow my gender to prevent you from reading further. You may have some very strong feelings about me because of past treatment from men or perhaps how your father raised you. Many men do not have a good record when it comes to our treatment of others.

I am writing to you because I am one who pressured someone much like you into having an abortion. I made sure she knew I would not be there for her and the baby if she chose to have it. I never gave her one ounce of hope that I could be swayed to commit to her or the child that I had helped to create.

I became an iron wall of resistance to any thought of becoming a responsible man, husband, or father. Even the idea of her having the baby and placing it up for adoption was an insult to the plans I had contrived for myself. That wonderful young lady and that baby growing in her womb were of little significance to me, compared to the grand plans I had for myself. I wanted this inconvenience out of the way and did everything I could to insure that the abortion took place. It did, and although I have received Christ's forgiveness that has freed me from this horrible choice, to this day I live with a painful regret that my child, our children, never was and never will be.

When I have spoken about the abortion to other men, they have often told me about their experiences. Some have wept openly in my arms. They too have feelings of doubt, regret, and shame. They have paid a stiff penalty for a choice that is so easily made in haste. They too have expressed their desire to undo the unimaginable. Like me they now look forward to a day in heaven when they can be with the child that was meant to be, but never was. The fellowship of their suffering is little comfort to me. It is only confirmation that many men like me owe women like you a great debt of apology and need to make restitution.

I write these words as a small offering to you from all men who shirked their duty and lived the life of common irresponsibility. Please forgive us where we have failed you.

God will restore you and renew your strength. You can trust God with your pain, your fears, and your future. When you experience His grace, you will be surprised by God. You will be amazed at His strength and astounded by His gentleness.

My hope for you is that *Her Choice to Heal* has been a book of truth and healing. I pray that you have found a new life and future in the arms of a God of not just second chances, but One of third, fourth, fifth chances and beyond. I pray that you will move beyond what you have done and into what God can do through you. Take the comfort you have been given and commit your life to dispersing comfort to those who find themselves locked in similar situations.

Truth with grace from the God who has loved even the thought of you for millions of years.

a final note

Sydna Massé
President
Ramah International, Inc.

When Joan and I began writing this book in 1997, we were convinced that it could offer a tangible hope to women struggling from post-abortion pain. But God laid it upon my heart that this book was only the first step—much more needs to be accomplished to reach post-abortive hearts with the hope of God's healing.

Following His call, in June of 1998, I left my position as manager of Focus on the Family's Crisis Pregnancy Ministries to begin a new ministry called Ramah International, Inc. This ministry is based on Jeremiah 31:15-17:

"A voice is heard in Ramah—mourning and great weeping—Rachel weeping for her children and refusing to be comforted because her children are no more" (verse 15).

As we have said in this book, the Alan Guttmacher Institute states that "at current rates, 43 percent of women have experienced abortion at least once by the age of forty-five."[1] While this is obviously a large segment of our society, these women are unnoticed because they refuse to reveal that abortion has happened in their lives. Many deny comfort because they fear rejection and are unable to confront their own part in ending their child's death. Except for a handful of small ministry efforts, little is being done to reach these hearts with the forgiveness and healing comfort available through Jesus Christ.

"This is what the Lord says—'restrain your voice from weeping and your eyes from tears. For your work will be rewarded—your children will return from the land of the enemy" (verse 16).

This is Ramah International's purpose—to bring post-abortive individuals (mothers, fathers, grandparents, and siblings) to healing so they can cease mourning, grieve these children's death, and become active participants in the pro-life movement. It is heartbreaking work to touch this pain, yet helping women to acknowledge the loss of their child is the first step toward healing, and their "work will be rewarded." By naming these aborted children, they become a permanent and tangible entity in the mother's heart. In essence, they are redeemed from Satan's grasp and "return from the land of the enemy."

"So their is hope for your future, says the Lord" (verse 17a).

What is our hope? For many of us the hope is to stop abortion from devastating other lives. I believe that it is only through our healed voices of abortion's devastation that this evil can be ended in our world. We are the only ones who can attest to the fact that abortion is a horrible choice—not only for the child be also for the woman.

Ramah International's objectives include: resource development, training programs on post-abortion ministry development, research on post-abortive issues, generation of awareness in American society of the post-abortive situation, and, finally, offering ministry services to other countries where an estimated 50,000,000 abortions occur each year.[2]

Call or write to find out how you can help us reach these hearts and be part of the solution to the abortion issue today. Call at (941)

473-2188, or write to: Ramah International, 1776 Hudson St., Englewood, FL 34223.

It is my sincere hope that God has used this book to open your heart to the wonders of His grace. May He bless you greatly as you continue to seek Him.

post-abortion resources

Organizations

Care Net

—A national affiliate organization, sponsoring hundreds of crisis pregnancy centers, providing training, materials for diverse ministries of each pregnancy center, including post-abortion support groups.

"Forgiven and Set Free" Bible Study
109 Carpenter Dr., Suite 100
Sterling, VA 20164
(703) 478-5661

Ramah International

—A national clearinghouse for post-abortion ministries, providing resources, referrals to the post-abortive women who call in. Also provides training workshops for post-abortion support group facilitators.

1776 Hudson St.,
Englewood, FL 34223
(941) 473-2188
www.ramahinternational.org

Heartbeat International

—A national affiliate organization of hundreds of crisis pregnancy centers, providing training, resources, and materials for the many ministries of each center, including post-abortion outreach.

7870 Olentangy River Rd., Suite 304
Columbus, OH 43235
(614) 885-7577, (888) 550-7577

National Institute for Family and Life Advocates (NIFLA)

—A national affiliate organization specializing in legal counsel and direction on how centers can become medical clinics. Supplies materials and resources for the many ministries of centers.

P.O. Box 42060
Fredricksburg, VA 22404
(540) 785-9853

National Office of Post-Abortion Reconciliation and Healing

—A national Catholic organization created to provide healing for the post-abortive, Catholic woman. Includes training for facilitating a post-abortion support group called Project Rachel, as well as materials and resources

3501 S. Lake Drive
Milwaukee, WI 53207
(800) 5WE-CARE

Books

Boundaries
Henry Cloud and John Townsend
Zondervan Books

Changes That Heal
Henry Cloud
Zondervan Books

Door of Hope
Jan Frank
Here's Life Publishers

Healing for Damaged Emotions
David Seamands
Chariot Victor Publishing

Hope, Help and Healing
Gregory Jantz
Harold Shaw Publishers

I'll Hold You in Heaven
Jack Hayford
Regal Books

In the Arms of God
James Dobson
Tyndale House Publishers

Lighting Mary's House
Lori Mitchell
Lighting Hearts Ministry
P.O. Box 63163
Colorado Springs, CO 80962

Making Abortion Rare
David Reardon
The Elliott Institute
P.O. Box 7348
Springfield, IL 62791

Reconcilable Differences
Jim Talley
Thomas Nelson Publishers

Shaping a Woman's Soul
Judith Couchman
Zondervan Publishers

Tilly
Frank Peretti
Crossway Publishers

Unlocking Childhood Memories
Kevin Leman and Randy Carlson
Thomas Nelson Publishers

endnotes

PROLOGUE

1. Anne C. Speckhard and Vincent M. Rue, "Post-Abortion Syndrome: An Emerging Public Health Concern," *Journal of Social Issues*, 48, no. 3 (1992).

CHAPTER 2

1. Frederica Matthewes-Green, *Policy Review*, Summer (1991).
2. Speckhard and Rue, "Post-Abortion Syndrome."
3. Paul and Teri Reisser, *Help for the Post Abortive Woman* (Lewiston, NY: Life Cycle Books, 1989) p.35.
4. Speckhard and Rue, "Post-Abortion Syndrome."

CHAPTER 3

1. Speckhard and Rue, "Post-Abortion Syndrome."
2. C.S. Lewis, *The Four Loves* (New York: Harcourt Brace Jovanovich, Inc., 1960) p.169.
3. Planned Parenthood New Mexico, *Newsletter,* summer (1996).
4. Mark Crutcher, *Lime 5, Exploited by Choice* (Denton, TX: Life Dynamics, 1996) p. 12.
5. William Morris, ed., *The American Heritage Dictionary, New College Edition* (Boston: Houghton Miflin Co., 1981) p. 1190.
6. Linda Cochrane, *Forgiven and Set Free Bible Study* (Grand Rapids, MI: Baker Book House, 1986, 1991, 1996) p.41.

7. Speckhard and Rue, "Post-Abortion Syndrome."
8. Linda Cochrane, *Forgiven and Set Free Bible Study,* p. 44.

CHAPTER 4

1. H. Norman Wright, *Crisis Counseling* (city:Regal Books) p. 285.
2. Ibid.
3. Speckhard and Rue, "Post-Abortion Syndrome."
4. Chapter 6, "The Heart of the Matter: Forgiveness" also deals with anger.

CHAPTER 6

1. *The American Heritage Dictionary*, p. 515.
2. C.S. Lewis, *Letters to Malcolm: Chiefly on Prayer* (New York: Harcourt Brace Jovanovich, Inc., 1964), p. 27.

CHAPTER 7

1. Frank Peretti, *Tilly* (Westchester, IL: Crossway Books, 1988)
2. Copyright © 1996 Sony/ATV Songs LLC, Sony/ATV Tunes LLC and Molto Bravo Music, Inc. All rights administered by Sony/ATV Music Publishing, 8 Music Square West, Nashville, TN 37203. All rights reserved, used by permission.
3. John W. Peterson, "Heaven Came Down," (John W. Peterson Music Co.: 1961, 1989). Used by permission.

CHAPTER 8

1. *Facts in Brief* (Alan Guttmacher Institute: January, 1997).

A FINAL NOTE

1. *Facts in Brief* (Alan Guttmacher Institute: January, 1997).
2. *Facts in Brief,* "Induced Abortion" (Alan Guttmacher Institute: January, 1991).

LIVING
BEYOND
REGRETS
You Can't Change Your Circumstances,
But God Can Change You!
GUY RICE DOUD

And these great titles. . .

Made Perfect in Weakness
by Gary Oliver
ISBN: 1-56476-719-1

This book helps Christians see failure as God sees failure–as a stepping stone to spiritual growth. Although spiritual people do "fail," the author guides us through the practical lessons that God seeks to teach us.